考古古龙州

Longzhou in the Archaeological Perspective

杨清平　李　敏　编著
Compiled by Yang Qingping　Li Min

广西科学技术出版社

图书在版编目（CIP）数据

考古龙州：汉英对照/杨清平，李敏编著. —南宁：广西
科学技术出版社，2017.11
ISBN 978-7-5551-0886-3

Ⅰ.①考… Ⅱ.①杨… ②李… Ⅲ.①考古发掘—概况
龙州县—汉、英 Ⅳ.①K872.674

中国版本图书馆 CIP 数据核字（2017）第 268539 号

考古龙州
KAOGU LONGZHOU

杨清平　李　敏　编著

钟　婕　黄艺平　翻译

责 任 编 辑：罗煜涛　　　　　　　　责 任 校 对：邓茹今
装 帧 设 计：韦娇林　　　　　　　　责 任 印 制：韦文印

出　版　人：卢培钊　　　　　　　　出版发行：广西科学技术出版社
社　　　址：广西南宁市东葛路 66 号　邮 政 编 码：530022
网　　　址：http://www.gxkjs.com

经　　　销：全国各地新华书店
印　　　刷：广西昭泰子隆彩印有限责任公司
地　　　址：南宁市友爱南路 39 号　　邮 政 编 码：530001
开　　　本：889 mm×1194 mm　1/16
字　　　数：230 千字　　　　　　　　印　　　张：10
版　　　次：2017 年 11 月第 1 版　　印　　　次：2017 年 11 月第 1 次印刷
书　　　号：ISBN 978-7-5551-0886-3
定　　　价：98.00 元

本书为2017年国家社科基金项目《左江花山岩画与相关考古遗存的关联性研究》（项目批准号：17XKG001）阶段性研究成果之一。

The present monograph is accrued to the phased development of the project *Research on Relationship between Zuojiang River Huashan Rock Art and the Archaeological Findings in the Area* sponsored by National Social Science Foundation（NO.17XKG001）in 2017.

作者简介

杨清平，男，汉族，出生于广西资源县，1994年北京大学考古系毕业，现为广西文物保护与考古研究所研究员。

已从事考古工作20多年，先后主持和参加了几十项田野调查和发掘工作。主持了多项国家级和自治区级课题，尤其是近年来主持完成了多项有关左江花山岩画文化景观申报世界文化遗产的考古课题，并取得重要成果，有力地推动了申遗工作的开展。发表和出版了学术论文和著作近40篇（部），在广西的史前考古、青铜时代考古以及地方史研究等方面有较深的造诣。

李敏，女，壮族，出生于广西龙州县，广西艺术学院音乐教育硕士研究生毕业，北京大学考古文博学院研修班毕业，现为龙州起义纪念馆馆长、龙州县博物馆馆长。自从事文博工作以来，在博物馆管理与研究方面成果丰硕，主持和参与了当地多项课题研究及多部著作的编写。

Profile of the Authors

Yang Qingping, male, Han nationality, born in Ziyuan county, graduated from Archaeology Department of Peking University in 1994. Yang serves as the researcher of Guangxi Institute of Cultural Relics Protection and Archaeology and the director of archaeological excavation now.

In the past more than 20 years, Yang has presided over a number of national and provincial projects, especially in recent years he has presided and participated in dozens of field investigation and excavation of which much concerned the research of Zuojiang River Huashan Rock Art Cultural Landscape, which facilitated the world cultural heritage application. Nearly forty theses and monographs have been published under his leading. Specilized in prehistoric age, bronze age and local history of Guangxi, he has contributed to cultural heritage conservation and archaeology development in the region.

Li Min, female, Zhuang nationality, born in Longzhou county, graduated from Guangxi Arts University with a master degree of music education major, graduate school of archaeology and culture in Peking University. She now serves as the curator of Longzhou Uprising Memorial Museum and Longzhou Museum, with considerable experiences and achievements in culture-related work. She has presided over quite a few research projects and boasted many monographs under her leading.

前言

　　龙州，位于广西壮族自治区西南部左江上游，距广西壮族自治区首府南宁市约200千米，东邻崇左市江州区，南接宁明县、凭祥市，东北与大新县相连，西北与越南接壤，总面积2317.8平方千米，总人口27万，有壮、汉、瑶、苗、回、侗等民族，壮族人口占总人口的95%。境内气候暖和湿润，自然风光秀丽，地质景观独特，民族文化丰富多彩。

　　龙州历史悠久，文化底蕴深厚。最新考古发现表明，距今8000年左右（属于新石器时代中期）就有人在这片土地上生产、生活，以后各朝各代都有人在此生息繁衍，留下了众多文物古迹。左江花山岩画、小连城、法国领事馆等名胜古迹更是龙州亮丽的名片。

　　为推进左江花山岩画文化景观申报世界文化遗产工作，广西文物保护与考古研究所受自治区文化厅、文物局委托，从2010年开始对左江流域进行了全面、细致的考古调查，其中在龙州发现了近20处遗址。至此，龙州境内发现的考古遗址达30多处。考古人员在调查的基础上选取龙州宝剑山A洞遗址、无名山遗址、大湾遗址、

坡叫环遗址、庭城遗址、舍巴遗址、沉香角遗址进行了试掘，发现了一大批重要遗迹和遗物。其中，有些遗物是在广西首次发现，引起了有关领导、专家、媒体和社会大众的广泛关注。这些发现不仅反映了龙州历史的悠久，而且体现了龙州古代历史文化面貌的独特性，同时有力推动了左江花山岩画文化景观申遗工作，为进一步研究龙州考古学文化内涵和年代序列等问题提供了珍贵的材料，具有重要意义。

近年来，笔者一直在左江流域主持花山岩画文化景观申报世界文化遗产的考古工作，对左江流域尤其是龙州考古有着比较全面的认识，经常被龙州的历史和文化所感动。为展示龙州悠久的历史，宣传龙州文物工作取得的巨大成就，促进龙州文化建设大发展、大繁荣，笔者将龙州考古所取得的一些重要成果进行初步整理，以图片加简要文字的形式编辑成这本册子。我们希望通过这种方式，让大家了解古代龙州，增强龙州人的自豪感和自信心，也为宣传龙州、建设"文化龙州"贡献我们微薄的力量。

Preface

Situated in the southwest part of the upper reaches of Zuojiang river, Longzhou county is about 200 kilometers away from Nanning, the capital city of Guangxi Zhuang Autonomous Region. Adjacent to the Jiangzhou district of Chongzuo city, south of Ningming county and Pingxiang city, northeast of Daxin county and northwest to Vietnam on the east, south, northeast and northwest respectively. It boasts a land area of 2317.8 square kilometers and a population of 2.7 million comprising of the nationalities of Zhuang, Han, Yao, Miao, Hui and Dong, of which the Zhuang nationality accounts for 95%. Longzhou county is blessed with warm and mild climate, picturesque scenery and geological landscapes as well as splendid ethnic culture.

Longzhou enjoys a time-honored history with profound cultural heritage, which finds testimony in the latest archaeological findings that people lived in this area as early as the mid neolithic age about 8000 years ago, such cultural and historical heritages as Zuojiang Huashan rock paintings, Xiaoliancheng as well as remains of the French Consulate bespeaks the beauty of Longzhou.

As part of the endeavor to promote the world cultural heritage application of Zuojiang River Huashan Rock Art Cultural

Landscape, on the commission of Department of Culture of Guangxi and Administration of Cultural Heritage of Guangxi, since 2010, Guangxi Institute of Cultural Relics Protection and Archaeology had carried out extensive archaeological research in the Zuojiang basin area which led to the discovery of about 20 archaeological sites in Longzhou county. More than 30 archaeological sites have been found in Longzhou. Archaeological sites of Cave A of Baojian Mountain, Wuming Mountain, Dawan, Pojiaohuan, Tingcheng, Sheba, Chenxiangjiao were excavated, with a great amount of relics of significance discovered among which were first of their kinds to be excavated in Guangxi. The findings shed light on the features of ancient Longzhou and facilitated the application. They are of significance in the archaeological research in Longzhou in terms of chronology definition and cultural profundity.

Recent years, we have witnessed my endeavor to promote world cultural heritage application of Huashan Rock Art Cultural Landscape and have been engaged in archaeological research in Longzhou county, which with its significant history and culture touched us dearly. The present brochure with pictures as well as explanatory words is devoted to the introduction of the archaeological research conducted in Longzhou county, which reflects on the great strides made in cultural development in the region.

In this way, we hope to learn about the ancient dragon state, strengthen the pride and self-confidence of Longzhou people, and also contribute to the promotion of Longzhou and the construction of *cultural dragon state.*

目 录

Contents

壹

龙州古代遗址分布概况

Part One　A Survey of Archaeological Sites in Longzhou

到目前为止，龙州境内共发现各类古文化遗址30多处，主要集中在左江及其支流丽江两岸。遗址的类型多种多样，按照地理位置来分，包括洞穴遗址、台地遗址、山坡遗址等；按照遗址性质来分，包括贝丘遗址、岩洞葬、城址、土坑墓等。遗址的时代从新石器时代中期延续到明清时期。这些遗址不仅类型多样，延续时间长，而且内涵也很丰富，反映了龙州延绵不断的历史发展，是龙州民族文化的重要组成部分。

More than thirty archaeological sites have been discovered in Longzhou county, most of which were located along Zuojiang river and its branch Lijiang river and came in various types. In terms of geographical location, they can be classified as cave sites, mesa sites and slope sites. They can also be categorized as shell moulds, cliff cave burial grounds, ancient city-sites and cave burial grounds in accordance with the nature of the site. The ages of these archaeological sites were expended from the neolithic age to the Ming and Qing dynasties.They were rich in forms and cultural significance, mirroring the continuous historical development of Longzhou.

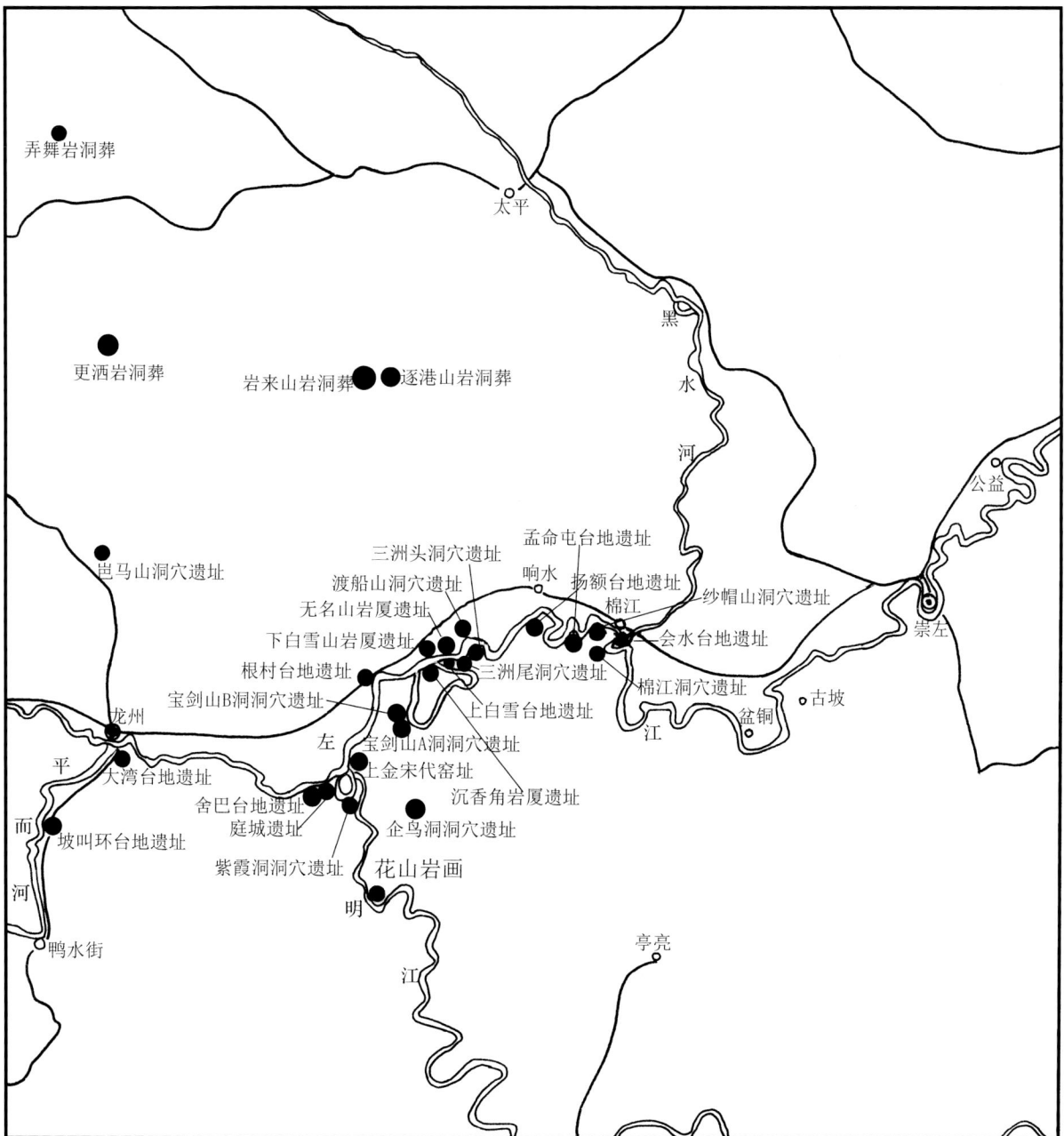

龙州县主要古遗迹分布示意图 Diagram of Major Archaeological Sites in Longzhou

主要考古遗存
Part Two　Major Archaeological Remains

一、龙州宝剑山A洞遗址

宝剑山A洞遗址位于广西壮族自治区崇左市龙州县上金乡两岸村小岸屯左江右岸、宝剑山岩画南面崖壁下约15米的岩洞内，北距宝剑山B洞遗址约80米。遗址所处的宝剑山为南北向的峰丛，东面临江，隔江为左江江岸一级台地。

遗址洞口距2013年洪汛期最高水位约10米，东南朝向。洞内面积约120平方米，分为外洞和内洞。

该遗址是2010年新发现的。为推进左江花山岩画文化景观申报世界文化遗产工作，2013年对其进行试掘，试掘面积20平方米。

宝剑山全景　Panaramic View of Baojian Mountain

Ⅰ. Archaeological Site of Cave A of Baojian Mountain

Cave A of Baojian Mountain is located in a cave on the cliff of Baojian Mountain in the Xiao'an hamlet of Liang'an village of Shangjin township in Longzhou county, about 80 meters to the north of which is Cave B Baojian Mountain Ranges face the north-south and are adjacent to the river on the east. In between the mountains are level Ⅰ mesa along the Zuojiang river.

The opening of the cave faces the southeast and is about 10 meters above the maximum flood line in 2013. The interior land area is 120 square meters.

It was discovered in 2010. 20 square meters of trial excavation was carried out in 2013 as part of the application of Zuojiang Huashan Rock Art Cultural Landscape as World Cultural Heritage.

宝剑山A洞遗址洞口
Entrance of Cave A
of Baojian Mountain

现场调查 Field Work

现场调查 Field Work

发掘现场 Excavation

现场讨论 Field Discussion

筛选 Sieving

遗址文化层堆积丰富，保存现状较好，最厚达250厘米。试掘区域地势由西向东倾斜，根据土质、土色及包含物自上而下共分九层。

初步分析，宝剑山A洞遗址可以分为两期。两个时期的文化大致衔接。

1.第一期遗存

第一期遗存遗迹主要包括三座墓葬和两处红烧土堆积。墓葬保存基本完整，不见墓坑，均为屈肢葬。两处红烧土均厚5～10厘米，土色呈暗红色，土质结构结实，包含物主要有少量螺蚌壳和烧骨。

T1南壁剖面 The Intersection of the South Side of the Cliff T1

The cultural layers of the site were in relatively sound keeping with rich cultural information, with the deepest layer amounting to 250 centimeters. The trial excavated area was on a west—to—east slope and nine—layered in accordance with the properties, color and the contents of the soil. Preliminary analysis had resulted in the conclusion that Cave A was developed in two successive periods the two periods of culture are almost lonnected.

1.The Remains of the First Period

The remains of the first period included three burials and two moulds of burned red clay. The burial remains were intact and in bent double position. The two moulds of burned red clay with thickness varying from 5 to 10 centimeters were dull red in color, compact in tissue and with some clam shells and burnt bones inside.

M1

M2

M3

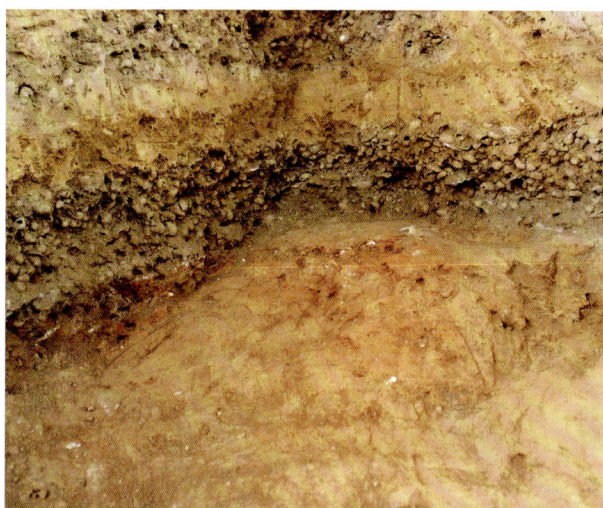
1号红烧土遗迹 NO.1 Site of Burned Red Clay Mould

2号红烧土遗迹 NO.2 Site of Burned Red Clay Mould

遗物

  宝剑山A洞遗址第一期遗存遗物包括石制品和蚌器。石制品原料均为砾石，岩性包括辉绿岩、硅质岩、石英等。器类包括打制石制品、磨制石制品和加工工具。其中，斧锛类器物先对砾石原料四周进行打制再磨刃口的做法很有地方特色。

砍砸器 Choppers

刮削器 Scraper

石片 Flake

Relics

Relics from Cave A of Baojian Mountain included stone implements and clam shell implements. The stone implements were made of gravel, including dolerite, chert and quartz and categorized as forged, polished, and processing tools. The excavated axes and adzes were made in such a particular way that the gravel raw material was forged wholly first and then the edge was polished.

斧锛类毛坯 Rough Casts of Axes or Adze

研磨器毛坯 Rough Cast of Stone Polishing Implement

　　蚌器有鱼头形穿孔蚌器、双肩蚌铲、锯齿刃蚌器等。双肩蚌铲不仅数量多，而且形制丰富，制作精美，锯齿刃蚌器在广西古代遗址中为首次发现。

The excavated clam shell implements came in the forms of pierced fish head-shaped implements, shoulder-shaped shovels and implements with serrated edge. The second of which were numerous, rich in forms and delicately made and were excavated for the first time within the ancient sites of Guangxi.

双肩蚌铲 The Shoulder-shaped Clam Shell Shovel

双肩蚌铲 The Shoulder-shaped Clam Shell Shovels

锯齿刃蚌器 Serrated-edged Clam Shell Implements

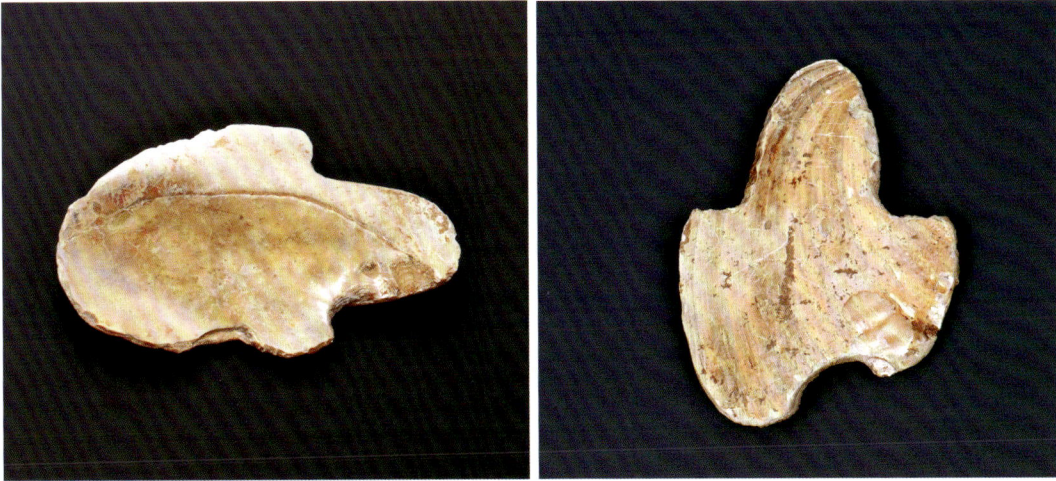

双肩蚌铲 The Shoulder-shaped Clam Shell Shovels

鱼头形穿孔蚌器 Pierced Fish Head-shaped Implement

2.第二期遗存

宝剑山A洞遗址第二期遗存为灰色堆积，含沙量大，有大量的人类骨骸。

（1）遗迹

从第②至第③层内大量人骨分布的情况来看，该地应该是一处岩洞葬。由于水浸等原因，人骨扰乱及腐朽十分严重，看不清完整个体。从残碎的骨骸初步判断，可能有9个个体。

（2）遗物

出土器物包括陶片、石器、蚌器、骨器等类别，以陶片为主。

石器均属于磨制石制品，包括石斧、石锛等类型。其中，双肩石斧通体精磨，制作精美，不见使用痕迹。

双肩石器 The Shoulder-shaped Stone Implement　　　　磨制石锛 Polished Stone Adze

2.The Remains of the Second Period

The remains of the second period were grey moulds, with large amount of sands and human skeletons.

（1）Remaining Site

The scattering skeletons indicated that it was a cave burial site. Owing to such geological conditions as water-soaking, the skeletons were in a highly decomposed condition and difficult to discern. It was judged that there were nine persons.

（2）Relics

The excavated items included ceramic flakes and implements made of stones, clam shells and bones, most of which were ceramic flakes.

The excavated stone implements including axes and adzes were polished, of which the delicately made shoulder-shaped stone axes were polished in full and seemed to be unused.

磨制石锛 Polished Stone Adze

陶片数量多，器型有釜、罐、碗、钵等，主要以夹砂釜罐类为主，大部分为圜底器。大多数为夹细砂、螺蚌壳粉陶，不见泥质陶。陶色不均。纹饰以细绳纹为主，见少量刻划的曲折纹、"S"形纹。少量陶器表面施薄陶衣，部分陶器底部、腹部有烟熏的使用痕迹，个别陶器内壁有疑似残留物的痕迹。

There were a large number of ceramic flakes, some with thin pottery coating from kettles, jars, bowls and pots were excavated, most of which were of sand, clam shell powder and with a round bottom, decorated with thin-rope-like patterns, carved zigzag pattern as well as *S* shape patterns. There were no clay ceramic and the color was nonuniform. Some pieces were tainted with smoke and leftovers, which bespoke their condition.

陶罐 Ceramic Jar

陶罐 Ceramic Jar

陶罐 Ceramic Jar

陶釜 Ceramic Kettles

陶釜 Ceramic Kettles

陶碗 Ceramic Bowl

陶碗 Ceramic Bowl

陶钵 Ceramic Pot

陶口沿 The Mouth of Ceramic Implement

蚌器主要有鱼头形蚌器、双肩蚌铲、束颈蚌铲等。

Implements made from clam shells excavated in this period included fish head-shaped clam shell implements, shoulder-shaped clam shell shovels, shoulder-shaped necked shovels, etc.

鱼头形蚌器 Fish Head–shaped Clam Shell Implement

双肩蚌铲 Shoulder–shaped Clam Shell Shovel

双肩蚌铲 Shoulder–shaped Clam Shell Shovel

束颈蚌铲 Shoulder–shaped Necked Shovel

骨器仅发现1件，为复式倒钩骨质剑形器，器型规整，造型精美，工艺细致。以动物肢骨磨制而成，短柄，束腰方格，长方形剑身，剑身两侧伸两组倒钩。此类骨器为广西先秦考古中首次发现。

The only bone piece excavated was delicately made from animal bone which was oblong with a short handle and two groups of barbs on the opposite sides of the blades. It was first of its kind to be excavated in Guangxi's archaeological research of the pre-Qin period.

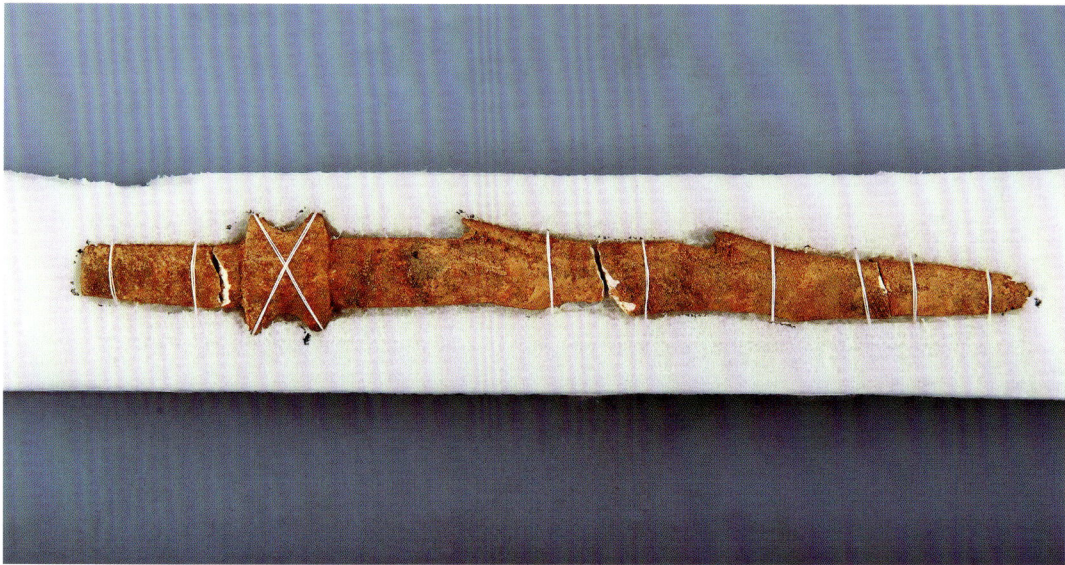

骨质剑形器 Bone Blade–like Implement

初步判断宝剑山A洞遗址第一期文化是一种带有显著地方特色的文化类型，第一期文化距今7000～4000年，第二期文化为商周时期。

宝剑山A洞遗址不仅堆积很厚，而且文化内涵丰富，具有重要的价值。

第一，该遗址上部的岩洞葬地层叠压在下部的新石器时代贝丘堆积之上，而且两期文化具有一定的延续性，这在广西还是第一次发现，为我们研究两者之间的关系提供了宝贵的资料，意义重大。

第二，从出土的遗物分析来看，宝剑山A洞洞穴遗址第一期文化与同期周边考古学文化面貌有很大不同，其地域特色明显，应该属于一个新的考古学文化类型。

第三，该遗址第二期遗存属于岩洞葬，出土的器物具有典型的地方特征，为研究古代骆越及其先民的文化提供了宝贵资料。

第四，岩洞葬与左江花山岩画均是骆越族群创造的杰作，两者族群的同一性无疑在这两种不同形态的物质文化之间建立了某种程度的联系，有助于我们研究岩画产生的历史背景。

第五，出土的骨质剑形器、锯齿刃蚌器都是广西考古第一次发现。

It was preliminarily estimated that Archaeological Site of Cave A of Baojian Mountain was developing in two periods: the first period being 7000 to 4000 years ago, and the second period being in the Shang and the Zhou Dynasties.

Archaeological Site of Cave A of Baojian Mountain was immense in volume and of significance with profound cultural value.

Firstly, burial mould was found to be laid on the shell mould from the Neolithic period, both of which were culturally connected and the first of its kind was discovered in Guangxi, which made valuable testimony to research in the relationship between the two.

Secondly, the relics were excavated from the first phase of the archaeological site of Cave A of Baojian Mountain differed greatly from the cultural features demonstrated by the archaeological excavation in the vicinity, which lent testimony to the fact that it was a new type of archaeological culture on its own.

Thirdly, the excavated implements from the second phase of this burial site were locally characteristic which would facilitate the research of the Luoyue people and their ancestors.

Fourthly, both the burial site and Huashan rock paintings along Zuojiang river were created by Luoyue people, which facilitated the research in the historical circumstance in which the rock paintings were created.

Fifthly, the excavated bone blade-like implements and the serrated-edged clam shell implements were unearthed for the first time in archaeological research in Guangxi.

时任国家文物局局长励小捷（右二）在参观遗址出土的器物 Li Xiaojie(second from right), the Then Director General of State Administration of Cultural Heritage Inspecting the Unearthed Relics

时任广西壮族自治区人民政府副主席李康（前排右一）等领导在听取遗址发掘情况汇报 Relevant Researchers Being debriefed by Li Kang(the front first from right), the Then Deputy Governor of Guangxi Zhuang Autonomous Region

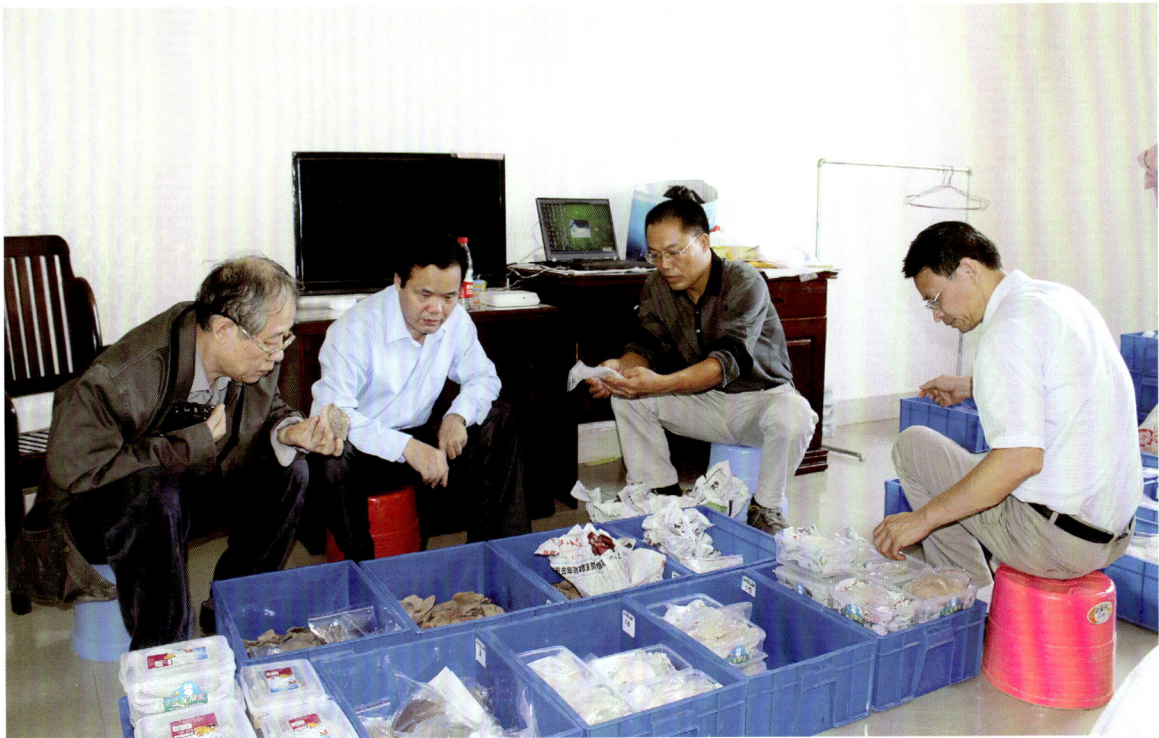

时任广西壮族自治区文化厅副巡视员谢日万（左二）在参观遗址出土的遗物   Xie Riwan(second from left), the then Associate Counsel of Department of Culture of Guangxi Zhuang Autonomous Region Inspecting the Unearthed Relics

考古龙州
Longzhou in the Archaeological Perspective

广西文物保护与考古研究所所长林强（左三）视察工地 Lin Qiang(third from left), Director of Guangxi Institue of Cultural Relics Protection and Archaeology Inspecting the Excavation Site

中国社会科学院考古研究所研究员傅宪国（左三）在发掘现场考察 Fu Xianguo(third from left), Researcher of the Institute of Archaeology of Chinese Academy of Social Sciences Inspecting the Excavation Site

广东五邑大学副校长张国雄（左一）等专家在发掘现场考察 Experts Including Zhang Guoxiong(first from left) Deputy, President of Wuyi University Inspecting the Excavation Site

龙州县主要领导参观遗址出土的遗物 Officials of Longzhou County Inspecting the Unearthed Relics

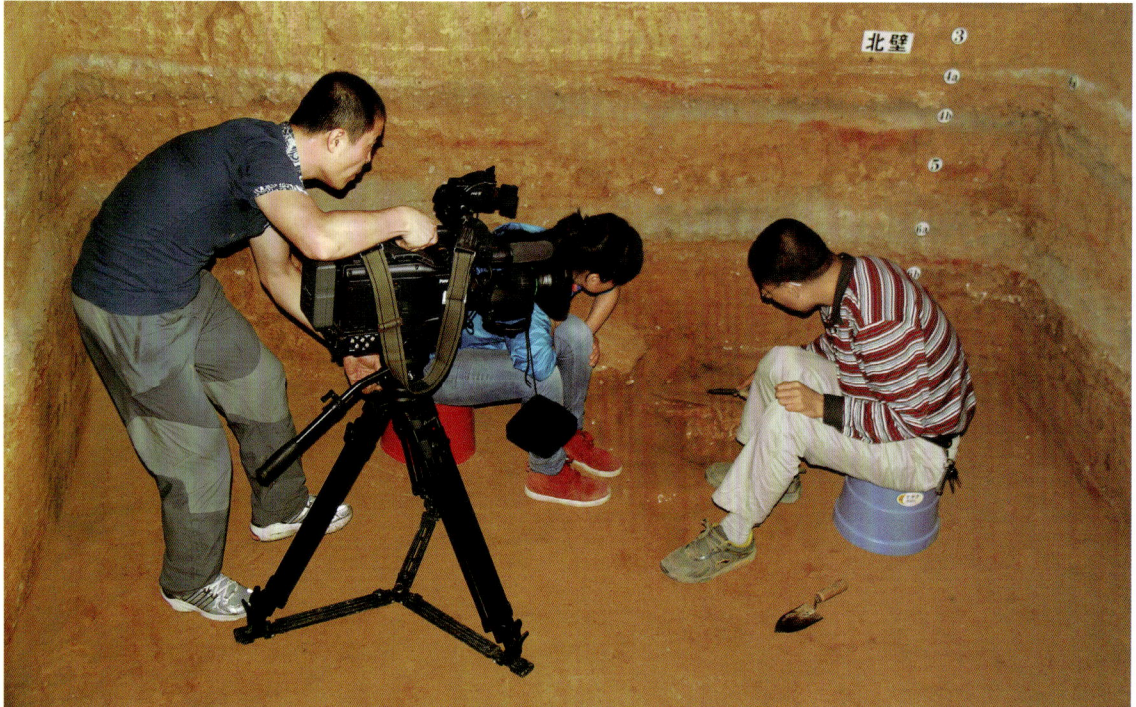

广西电视台记者在发掘现场进行采访 Journalists from GXTV Reporting on the Excavation

媒体记者在发掘现场进行采访 Journalists Reporting on the Excavation

二、舍巴遗址

舍巴遗址位于上金乡联江村舍巴屯东北约20米的丽江南岸台地上，丽江和明江在其北面约500米处汇入左江。遗址于2009年开展左江流域专题调查时被发现，其南北长约40米，东西宽约20米，分布面积约800平方米。遗址临江部位为石灰岩基础，结构较为稳定，整个堆积因山势自西面向江边倾斜，地表散布大量螺壳和石器。

Ⅱ. Archaeological Site of Sheba

The archaeological site of Sheba was situated on the mesa along the south bank of Lijiang river about 20 meters away to the northeast of Sheba district of Lianjiang village of Shangjin township, about 500 meters away to the north of where the Lijiang river and Mingjiang river converge into Zuojiang river. The site with a length of about 40 meters from north to south, and a width of about 20 meters from east to west, was discovered in a themed research on Zuojiang river basin in 2009. It was dispersed on an area of about 800 square meters and inclined to the west, with the part by the river being solid limestone basis and a large amount of clam shells and stone implements on the surface of the site.

遗址近景 Near View of the Site

2010年11～12月对其进行试掘，共布2米×5米探沟一条，发掘面积为10平方米。

The excavation of the site was conducted in a exploratory trench of 2 meters wide and 5 meters long from November to December in 2010, with an excavated area of 10 square meters.

探沟 Exploratory Trench

现场工作场景 Excavation

现场取样 Sampling

The site was excavated and showed six layers of moulds. 从发掘情况来看，遗址共有六层堆积。

南壁地层 The Intersection of the Moulds on the South Side

发掘共获取器物200多件，包括石器、骨器、陶器等，另外还出土大量动物标本及石器原料、断块、废料等石制品。

More than 200 pieces of relics were unearthed, including implements of stones, bones and ceramics, animal specimens, stone, broken chunks and clippings.

鹿角 Antlers

砍砸器 Choppers

砍砸器 Choppers

刮削器Scrapers

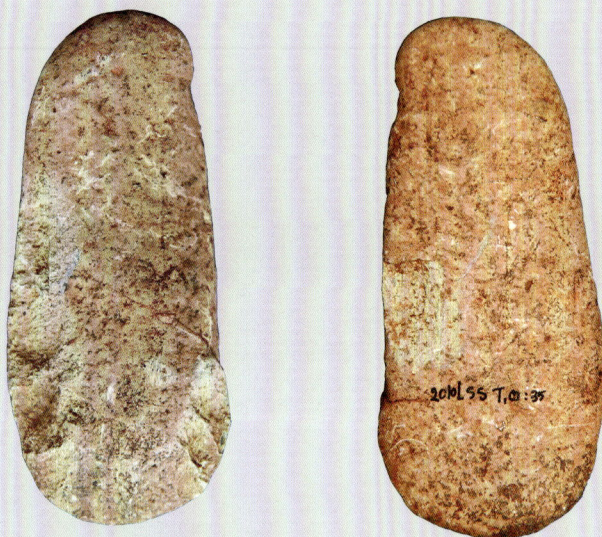

斧锛类毛坯 Rough Casts of Stone Axe or Adze

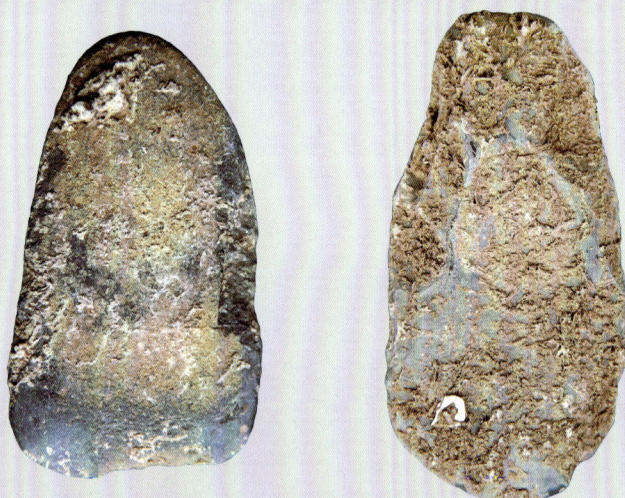

斧锛类半成品 Semi-finished Pieces of Axe or Adze

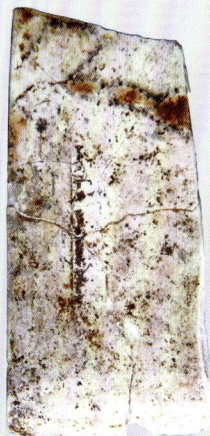

石锛　Stone Adzes

石锛　Stone Adzes

带切割痕石废料　Scratched Stone Clippings

石网坠 Stone Reticulated Pendant

砺石 Grinder

骨器 Bone Implement

根据地层堆积状况及包含物，舍巴遗址大致可分为三期。

第一期，以螺壳堆积为代表，出土少量打制石片石器及磨制石器，不见陶片。包含的动物骨骼是以水生的蚌壳、鱼类及龟鳖类为主，另外还有部分小型哺乳动物骨骼。这一时期人类生业模式是以捕捞业为主，从遗物特征看其年代距今大约7000年。

第二期，地层堆积包含螺壳较少，哺乳类动物骨骼较多，石制品以砍砸器及大型石片石器为主，同时还发现大量石器原料、断块、废料等。这一时期生业模式发生了改变，经济类型变成以狩猎为主。其年代距今7000～6000年。

第三期，地层堆积相对较为纯净，不含螺壳，除在本层表面有少量类似人类肢骨的痕迹外，不见任何骨骼，同时石器出土也较少，基本不见打制石器。这一时期石器在石料的选择方面较为讲究，主要选取类似于大理石一类的岩石进行切割之后再进行精磨。另外还出土了一件绳纹夹砂圜底罐残片。其年代为距今4000～3000年。

舍巴遗址地层堆积保存较好，系列较完整。这对于研究左江流域古代文化面貌、考古学文化发展序列、生业模式、环境气候等方面具有重要意义。

The excavated site was divided into three periods in accordance with the situation of the moulds and contents therein.

The first period was characteristic of clam shell mould with a small amount of forged stone flakes and polished stone implements, animal bones, most of which were aquatic animals and small mammals, without ceramics, which lent testimony to the fact that people in this period mainly lived on fishery. It was about 7000 years ago.

The second period was featured with a large amount of mammals bones and choppers and stone flakes. People in this period mainly lived on hunting. It was 7000 to 6000 years ago.

The mould of the third period was relatively purified without clam shells and hardly any forged stone implements and relics of bones except for some human limb bones. The stone implements of this phase were cut and polished from chosen marbles. A piece from a pot with sand, rope-pattern decoration and a round bottom was excavated. It was 4000 to 3000 years ago.

The archaeological site of Sheba was well preserved, which was of significance in research about the ancient culture, livelihood and climate in the Zuojiang river basin area as well as the archaeological chronology.

三、根村遗址

根村遗址位于广西壮族自治区崇左市龙州县上金乡进明村根村屯上游约1200米左江与勤江溪交汇处的左江左岸台地上。遗址东面、北面为甘蔗地，南面为左江，距江面约10米，西面为勤江溪，距水面约8米。遗址东西长约80米，南北宽约30米，分布面积约2400平方米。地表可见明显的螺壳、蚌壳，堆积厚0.5～2米。

该遗址于2014年12月被发现，2015年1～2月对其进行试掘，布1米×5米探沟两条，发掘面积10平方米。

遗址地貌 Landform of the Site

Ⅲ. Archaeological Site of Gencun

The archaeological site of Gencun was situated on the mesa along the left bank of Zuojiang river about 1200 meters away from the Gencun district of Jinming village of Shangjin township of Longzhou county, Chongzuo city, where Zuojiang river and Qinjiang brook converge. It was faced with sugarcanes fields on the east and north sides. Zuojiang river and Qinjiang brook were about 10 meters on the south side and about 8 meters on the west side respectively. With a length of about 80 meters from east to west and a width of about 30 meters from north to south, the site occupied an area of 2400 square meters with visible clam shells and snails layer which amounted to a thickness of 0.5 to 2 meters.

It was discovered in December in 2014. Exploratory excavation was carried out from January to February in 2015 in two exploratory trenches with a width of 1 meter and a length 5 meters, the excavation area was 10 square meters.

发掘现场 Excavation

发掘现场 Excavation

遗址堆积可分为七个文化层，均包含大量螺壳，各文化层均出土文化遗物。

发现的遗迹主要为墓葬。墓葬均找不到墓坑，大部分人骨保存较好。葬式包括侧身屈肢、仰身屈肢葬等，其中以仰身屈肢葬为主。

TG2东壁剖面 The Intersection of the East Side of the TG2

The excavated moulds were divided into seven layers, with a large amount of snail shells and cultural relics from every layer.

The excavation was mainly human remains without burial pits, in which most human bones were well preserved, in such positions of flexed limbs on one side or on the back, the latter of which was the main position.

墓葬 Human Remains

墓葬 Human Remains

遗址出土遗物200多件，包括打制石器、磨制石器、骨器、蚌器和大量水、陆生动物遗骸。石器中打制石器占绝大多数，打制石器以砍砸器、刮削器为主，制作简单。磨制石器较少，主要为磨制比较精细的斧、锛、研磨器等。另外，发现少量蚌器和骨器。水、陆生动物遗骸种类丰富，初步判断有20多种。

石片 Flake

石片 Flake

石片 Flake

石片 Flake

石片 Flake

More than 200 pieces of relics were unearthed, including forged stone implements, polished stone implements, bone implements, clam shell implements as well as a large amount of aquatic and terrestrial animals' bones. Most stone implements were forged ones made in a simple way such as choppers as well as scrapers. Only a few polished implements were unearthed, most of which were delicately made, such as axes, adzes and stone implements for polishing. A few clam shell implements and bone implements were also discovered. More than 20 kinds of aquatic and terrestrial animals' bones were excavated.

刮削器 Scraper

砍砸器 Chopper

砍砸器 Chopper

砍砸器 Chopper

研磨器毛坯 Rough Cast of Stone Implement for Polishing

研磨器毛坯 Rough Casts of Stone Implement for Polishing

石锛 Stone Adzes

石锛 Stone Adzes

石锛 Stone Adzes

石锛 Stone Adzes

石斧 Stone Axes

斧锛毛坯 Rough Casts of Stone Adze or Axe

斧锛毛坯 Rough Casts of Stone Adze or Axe

石锤 Hammer Stones

蚌铲 Clam Shell Shovel

　　从试掘所见的遗迹和遗物初步判断该遗址年代在距今5000～4000年，属于新石器时代中晚期。

　　It was estimated that the period was the latter half of the Neolithic period 5000 to 4000 years ago in accordance with the unearthed remains and relics from the exploratory excavation.

四、无名山遗址

无名山遗址位于广西壮族自治区崇左市龙州县上金乡卷逢村白雪屯对岸的无名山岩厦下，面积约600平方米。遗址地势由南向北倾斜，属于左江左岸一级台地，所处的山峰大致为东西走向，崖壁面向左江，距离地面20～30米处伸出一较为平整、宽约5米的天然石檐，可挡雨水。遗址距现江面高度约10米，西距上游的下白雪山岩画点500米，东距下游无名山岩画点约200米、距在建的白雪旅游码头约900米，南距隔江的白雪屯约950米，北距沥青村道约350米。

该遗址于2013年9月被发现，同年11～12月对其进行发掘。试掘位置位于遗址的中部，布5米×5米探方1个，正南北方向，实际发掘16平方米。

试掘区域地势由西向东倾斜，根据土质、土色及包含物判断遗址地层自上而下共分为四层，均含有螺壳。

出土文化遗物200多件，主要有石器、蚌器、铁器、骨器、陶片和水、陆生动物遗骸等。该遗址文化可以分为两期。

遗址地貌 Landform of the Site

Ⅳ. Archaeological Site of Wuming Mountain

With an area of about 600 square meters, the archaeological site of Wuming Mountain was located in the rock shelter of Wuming Mountain on the opposite of Baixue hamlet of Juanfeng village of Shangjin township of Longzhou county in Chongzuo city. The mesa on which the site was situated tilted from south to north, with the cliff facing Zuojiang river and a stone ceiling with a width of about 5 meters above about 20 to 30 meters from the river. The site was about 10 meters above the river, 500 meters from the west end to the Xiabaixue Mountain rock painting, 200 meters from the east end to the Wuming Mountain rock painting, about 900 meters from the tourism wharf in construction, about 950 meters from the south end to the Baixue hamlet on the opposite side, about 350 meters from the north end to the Liqing village.

It was discovered in September 2013 and excavated from November to December in the same year. The exploratory excavation was conducted in the middle of the site, with a trench of 5 meters wide and 5 meters long running from south to north. The excavated area was 16 square meters.

The excavated area was tilted from west to east. It was four-layered in accordance with the properties, color and contents of the soil, every layer containing snail shells.

More than 200 pieces of cultural relics were unearthed, including stone implements, clam shell implements, iron implements, bone implements, ceramic flakes, aquatic as well as terrestrial animals' remains, which were decided to have existed in two periods.

发掘现场 Excavation

T1西壁剖面 The Intersection of the West Side of the Cliff T1

59

1.第一期遗存

不见遗迹，遗物包括石器、蚌器等。

石器有打制和磨制两种。打制石器主要类型有砍砸器、刮削器、石核、石片等，以砍砸器为主，刮削器次之。砍砸器大部分用砾石直接打制且均为单面加工而成，器表大部分保留砾面，刃部有的具有明显的使用痕迹。刮削器大部分用砾石直接加工而成，器形较小，均为单边侧刃刮削器，器表大部分保留砾面。磨制石器主要类型有石锛、石斧及砺石。锛、斧类大部分用砾石直接磨制而成，器体较小，残段较多。磨制方式分为直接在刃部磨制、先琢打器物两侧及刃部边缘再磨刃部、先琢打刃部再磨刃部三类。砺石，已残，均为沙岩质，器表遗留有磨制石器的使用痕迹。

石片 Flakes

1. Remains of the First Period

No remains were identified in this phase. Relics unearthed included stone implements and clam shells implements.

The unearthed stone implements included forged ones and polished ones. Forged stone implements included choppers, scrapers, cores and flakes. The excavated forged stone implements, of which choppers were largest in number and scrapers were in second, most of which were made of gravel, were one-sided and retained with gravel surface. Polished stone implements came in the forms of adzes, axes and grinders. The axes and adzes were mostly made of gravel and small with broken pieces. The polished stone implements were made in the following three ways, namely polishing the edge, polishing the sides and the edge as well as forging and polishing the edge. Visible trace of usage were identified on the implements.

砍砸器 Choppers

刮削器 Scrapers

刮削器 Scrapers

石锛 Stone Adzes

石锛 Stone Adzes

石斧 Stone Axe

石锤 Hammer Stone

蚌器类型主要有穿孔蚌器、双肩蚌铲、锯齿刃蚌器、蚌刀、蚌器半成品及废料等。

陶片 Ceramic Flakes

锯齿刃蚌器 Serrated-edged Clam Shell Implement

锯齿刃蚌器 Serrated-edged Clam Shell Implement

Such clam shell implements as pierced clam shell implements, shoulder-shaped clam shell shovels, serrated-edged clam shell implements, clam shell knives, semi-finished clam shell implements as well as chippings were unearthed.

双肩蚌铲 Shoulder–shaped Clam Shell Shovel

穿孔蚌器 Pierced Clam Shell Implement

蚌刀 Clam Shell Knife

2.第二期遗存

不见遗迹，遗物有陶器、铁器以及少量的石器、蚌器和骨器。

石器、蚌器与第一期出土的同类器物差不多，骨器仅有1件骨针出土。

陶片均为夹砂陶，大部分烧制火候较低，有少量火候较高的硬陶。陶片有灰陶、红陶及黑陶，主要以灰陶、黑陶为主。根据陶片残段来看，器型以釜罐类为主，有圜底器，也有圈足器；绝大部分饰有纹饰，素面占少部分；纹饰主要以绳纹为主，有少量弦纹和"米"字纹。

铁器有两个残断的铁锸出土。

初步分析，第一期年代应属于新石器时代中晚期，距今5000年左右；第二期年代为汉代。

陶片 Ceramic Flakes

2. Remains from the Second Period

No human remains were unearthed but such relics as ceramic implements, iron implements, a few stone implements, clam shell implements as well as some bones implements were unearthed.

Similar stone implements and clam shell implements with those that had been excavated in the first phase were unearthed. One bone needle was unearthed.

Most unearthed ceramic flakes were coarse and fired in low temperature, a few of which were fired in relatively intensive heat and in grey and black and some of which were red. Most ceramic flakes were part of pots and jars which were round at the bottom and some with ring legs decorated with either rope pattern, string pattern or "米" pattern.

Two broken iron spades were excavated.

It was estimated that the first phase was about 5000 years ago in the latter half of the Neolithic period. The second phase was in the Han Dynasty.

陶片 Ceramic Flake

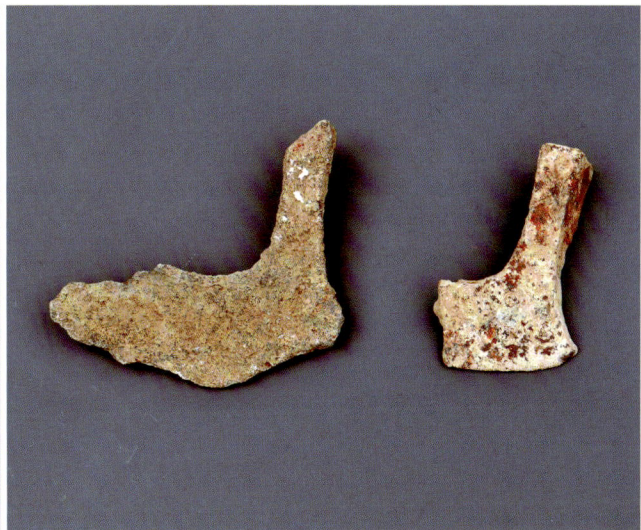

铁锸 Iron Spades

五、大湾遗址

大湾遗址位于广西壮族自治区崇左市龙州县龙州镇岭南村大湾屯东北约1000米处，左江上游（丽江段）右岸台地上一处坡地，西北方向与龙州纸厂隔江而望。遗址东、北两面紧邻丽江，距现江面高约15米；南面为甘蔗地；西面为一南北向冲沟。遗址南北长约50米，东西宽约13米，分布面积约400平方米，地表可见密集分布的螺壳、蚌壳。

2015年11～12月对该遗址进行试掘，试掘面积为32平方米。

遗址地貌 Landform of the Site

探方全景 General View of the Pit

V. Archaeological Site of Dawan

The archaeological site of Dawan was situated about 1000 meters to the northeast of Dawan district of Lingnan village of Longzhou township of Longzhou county in Chongzuo city. It rested on a slope of the mesa on the right bank of the upper reaches of Zuojiang river, being the opposite of Longzhou Paper-making Factory on the northwest. It was adjacent to the Lijiang river on the east and the north, to a sugarcane field on the south, a gully running from north to south on the west. The site was about 15 meters above river, with a length of about 50 meters from south to north, a width of about 13 meters from east to west and an area of 400 square meters. Serried snail and clam shells were dispersed on the surface.

Exploratory excavation was carried out from November to December in 2015, with an area of 32 square meters unearthed.

遗迹清理 Trained Personnel at work（sorting out the relics）

筛选 Sieving

遗址保存状况较好，堆积破坏较少，堆积深度达1.7米。根据土质、土色及包含物判断可以分为十层，每层都含有一定数量的螺壳。

The site was well-preserved. The mould, with a depth of 1.7 meters, could be divided into 10 layers in accordance with the properties, color and contents of the soil. Every layer of the mould was found to contain number of snail shells.

T1东壁剖面 The Intersection of the East Side of the Cliff T1

试掘发现的遗迹，主要有红烧土遗迹、灰坑和墓葬。

红烧土遗迹多集中分布，范围不大但堆积较厚，厚5～8厘米，往往夹杂少量炭屑，应为人类用火的遗迹现象。

灰坑平面形状多呈圆形或椭圆状，多为弧壁圜底，坑壁面较光滑，直径约1米，深度为40～60厘米，内填土较为杂乱。

墓葬有2座，均未见墓圹，人骨保存状况较差，均为屈肢葬。

红烧土遗迹 Remains of Burnt Clay

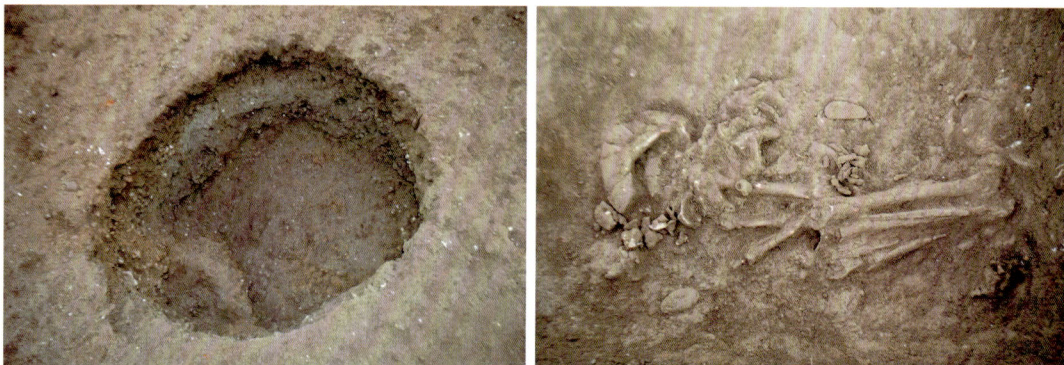

灰坑 Clay Pit

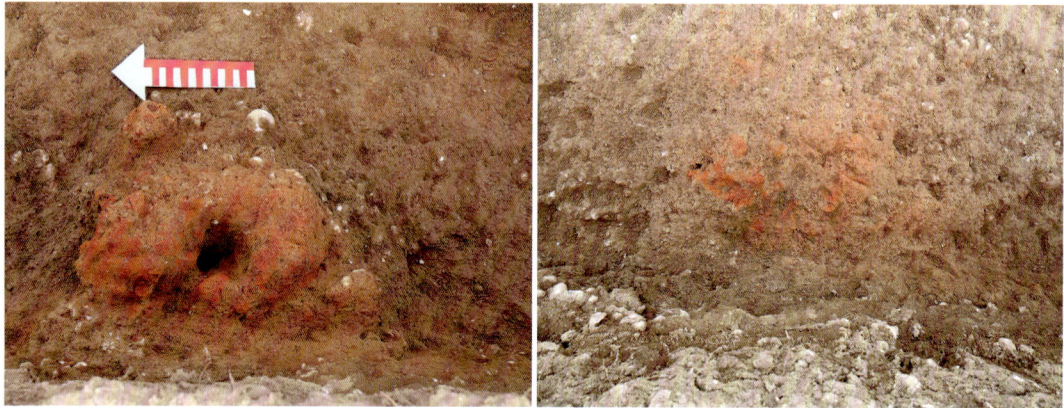

墓葬 Human Remains

Burnt clay relics, clay pits and burial ground were unearthed in the exploratory excavation.

Burnt clay relics with a thickness of about 5 to 8 centimeters clustered over a small area with traces of charcoal bits, which bespoke the employment of fire by people at that time.

Clay pits, with a diameter of about 1 meter and a depth of 40 to 60 centimeters, were mostly round or oval with round bottom and the interior wall was halved and smooth. The filling soil was consorted.

Two human remains were unearthed without burial grounds, the human bones were in poor condition and flexed position.

出土遗物600多件，包括大量打制（磨制）石器，大量水、陆生动物碎骨和极少数蚌器。石器中打制石器占绝大多数，打制石器以砍砸器、刮削器为主，制作简单。磨制石器较少，主要为磨制比较精细的斧、锛。另外还有大量的断块和石锤，蚌器2件。水、陆生动物遗骸种类较为丰富，初步判断有猪、鹿、鼠、鱼等。

More than 600 pieces of relics were excavated, including a large amount of forged and polished stone implements, crushed bones of aquatic and terrestrial animals as well as a few clam shell implements. Most of the simply made stone implements were forged ones including choppers and scrapers. Polished stone implements were small in number in the forms of axe and adze. A large amount of broken stone implements and hammer stones as well as two clam shell implements were unearthed. The unearthed animal bones were varied in types, which, in accordance with the relics, were estimated to be pigs, deer, rats, fish, etc.

石核 Core

石核 Core

砍砸器 Chopper

砍砸器 Chopper

砍砸器 Chopper

砍砸器 Chopper

砍砸器 Chopper

砍砸器 Chopper

刮削器 Scraper

刮削器 Scraper

刮削器 Scraper

刮削器 Scraper

石片 Flake

石片 Flake

石片 Flake

石片 Flake

斧锛毛坯 Rough Cast of Stone Axe or Adze

斧锛毛坯 Rough Cast of Stone Axe or Adze

斧锛毛坯 Rough Cast of Stone Axe or Adze

斧锛毛坯 Rough Cast of Stone Axe or Adze

石凿毛坯 Rough Cast of Stone Chisel

石凿毛坯 Rough Cast of Stone Chisel

石凿 Stone Chisel

研磨器 Stone Implement for Polishing

研磨器毛坯 Rough Casts of Stone Implements for Polishing

研磨器毛坯 Rough Casts of Stone Implements for Polishing

石锛 Stone Adze

石锛 Stone Adze

石锛 Stone Adze

石锛 Stone Adze

石斧 Stone Axe

石斧 Stone Axe

石斧 Stone Axe

石斧 Stone Axe

石锤 Hammer Stone

石锤 Hammer Stone

石锤 Hammer Stone

石锤 Hammer Stone

蚌勺 Clam Shell Spoon

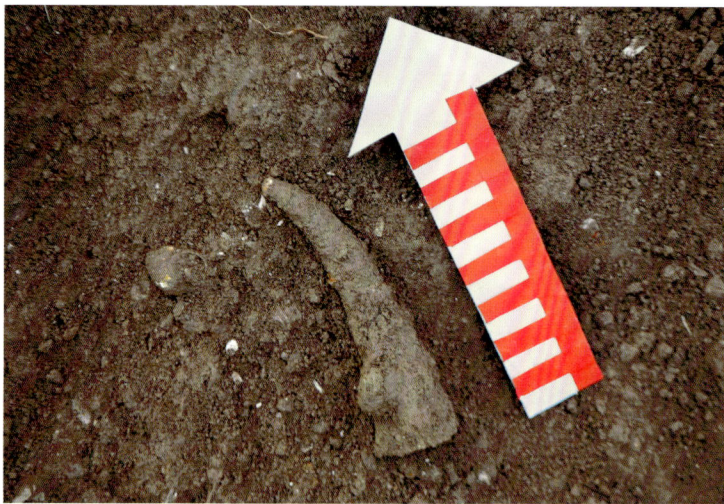

鹿角 Antler

　　从试掘所见的遗迹和遗物初步判断该遗址年代距今5000年左右，属于新石器时代中晚期。

It was estimated that the site was in the latter half of the Neolithic period which was about 5000 years ago in accordance with the unearthed remains and relics.

六、坡叫环遗址

　　坡叫环遗址位于广西壮族自治区崇左市龙州县上降乡里城村板色屯西北约500米平而河右岸小缓坡的西面坡上。遗址由一处略呈南北狭长状的土坡组成，地势稍陡，坡度约为40°，属左江河一级支流至平而河右岸的第二级阶地，高出左江河面约20米。遗址南北长约20米，东西宽约15米，分布面积约300平方米。

　　遗址地表可见大量密集堆积的螺、蚌壳，螺壳、蚌壳种类较为丰富，其中约90%的螺壳尾端均被敲掉。

　　该遗址于2015年被发现。为配合花山岩画文化景观申报世界文化遗产工作，广西文物保护与考古研究所于2015年12月至2016年1月对遗址进行小规模试掘，试掘面积为50平方米。

遗址地表螺壳堆积 The Serried Snail Shells on the Surface of the Site

VI. Archaeological Site of Pojiaohuan

The archaeological site of Pojiaohuan was situated on the west side of the gentle slope of the right bank about 500 meters to the northwest of Banse hamlet of Licheng village of Shangjiang township of Longzhou county in Chongzuo city. The site was on a long and narrow acute soil slope of about 40 degrees and about 20 meters above the Zuojiang river, with a length of about 20 meters from south to north, a width about 15 meters from east to west over an area of about 300 square meters. The slope was a mesa on the second level of the first level branch of Zuojiang river.

Serried snails and clam shells were dispersed on the site, which were varied in types, 90% of which were clipped off the ends.

The site was discovered in 2015. As part of the endeavor to apply for the Zuojiang River Huashan Rock Art Cultural Landscape as World Cultural Heritage, exploratory excavation was carried out by Guangxi Institute of Cultural Relics Protection and Archaeology from December 2015 to January 2016 on a small scale covering an area of 50 square meters.

探方分布 The Excavated Pits

发掘现场 Excavation

遺址保存状況较好，堆积破坏较少。堆积深度约1.5米，可分为15层，每层都含有大量螺壳。

The site was well-preserved. The moulds were in good condition with a depth of 1.5 meters and could be divided into 15 layers, every of which contained a great number of snails shells.

T1北壁剖面 The Intersection of the North Side of the Cliff T1

遗址发现小型石器加工坊1处、灰坑1处。

小型石器加工坊石器分布范围约1.4米×1.4米，石器分布密集，共计45件。以石片、断块为主，兼有部分石料、砍砸器、石核、石砧、石锤。以石砧为中心，石锤、石核、砍砸器、石片、断块等紧邻石砧。部分石器下直接叠压着一层厚约5厘米的灰烬堆积。灰烬包含大量炭屑和烧螺、烧骨。

灰坑平面呈椭圆形，正南北走向，剖面形状呈弧形平底，壁面光滑较缓，底面较为平缓，坑底石器分布密集，且部分磨制精美。

A small-scaled stone implement making mill and a grey clay pit were discovered.

The small-scaled stone implement making mill covered an area of about 1.4 m×1.4 m, with 45 implements dispersed in a serried manner, most of which were stone flakes and broken chunks as well as stones, choppers, cores, hammer stones and stone anvils which were situated in the center. Under some implement stones were ashes of about 5 centimeters comprising of charcoal, burnt snails shells and burnt bones.

The excavated clay pit was situated in a south-to-north manner, with an oval opening and an arc section, smooth and gentle wall, delicately made stone implements dispersed in a serried manner at the bottom.

小型石器加工坊 The Small-scaled Stone Implement Making Mill

灰坑 Clay Pit

坡叫环遗址出土遗物极其丰富，包括2000多件石器，200多件蚌器，若干骨椎，大量水、陆生动物遗骸。

出土物以石器为主，石器类型丰富，多为大石片石器，包括砍砸器、刮削器、石锤、石砧、砺石、研磨器、间打器、石斧、石锛、石核、石片、断块等。石器中打制石器占绝大多数，打制石器以砍砸器、刮削器为主，制作简单。磨制石器，包括石斧、石锛等。出土蚌器约200件，由晚及早，大小形制较为一致，多为一端稍凹的蚌勺。

A great number of relics were excavated in Pojiaohuan site, including more than 2000 pieces of stone implements, more than 200 clam shell implements, some vertebral bones, a large number of aquatic and terrestrial animals remains.

The excavated stone implements were varied in types, most of which were choppers, scrapers, hammer stones, stone anvils, grind stone, stones implement for polishing, stone tools, stone axes, stone adzes, cores, flakes and broken chunks. About 200 pieces of clam shell implements were excavated, which were uniform in size and most of them were in the shape of a spoon with a vortex.

窄槽砺石 Grind Stone with Narrow Grooves

窄槽砺石 Grind Stones with Narrow Grooves

砺石 Grind Stone

砺石 Grind Stone

石锤 Hammer Stone

石锤 Hammer Stone

石砧 Stone Anvil

石砧 Stone Anvil

石核 Core

石核 Core

石片 Flake

石片 Flake

石片 Flake

石片 Flake

刮削器 Scraper

刮削器 Scraper

刮削器 Scraper

刮削器 Scraper

砍砸器 Chopper

砍砸器 Chopper

砍砸器 Chopper

砍砸器 Chopper

砍砸器 Chopper

砍砸器 Chopper

石凿毛坯 Rough Cast of Stone Chisel

石凿 Stone Chisel

研磨器 Stone Implement for Polishing

研磨器 Stone Implement for Polishing

研磨器 Stone Implement for Polishing

研磨器 Stone Implement for Polishing

研磨器毛坯 Rough Cast of Stone
Implement for Polishing

研磨器毛坯 Rough Cast of Stone
Implement for Polishing

石锛 Stone Adze

石锛 Stone Adze

石锛 Stone Adze

石锛 Stone Adze

石锛 Stone Adze

石锛 Stone Adze

斧锛毛坯 Rough Cast of Stone Axe or Adze

斧锛毛坯 Rough Cast of Stone Axe or Adze

斧锛毛坯 Rough Cast of Stone Axe or Adze

斧锛毛坯 Rough Cast of Stone Axe or Adze

石斧 Stone Axe

石斧 Stone Axe

石斧 Stone Axe

石斧 Stone Axe

蚌勺 Clam Shell Spoon

蚌勺 Clam Shell Spoon

　　根据试掘所见的遗迹和遗物初步判断该遗址年代在距今8000～7000年，属于新石器时代中期。

　　坡叫环遗址的试掘出土了大量的石器和蚌器，石器类型较为丰富，还发现了左江流域首个小型石器加工坊。以大石片石器为主要风格的文化面貌与左江流域同时期其他遗址相比区别明显。该遗址不仅进一步补充了左江流域新石器时代的考古材料，还代表了左江流域新石器时代一种新的文化类型，意义重大。

　　The excavated site was from the middle of the Neolithic period which was 8000 to 7000 years ago in accordance with the relics and remains unearthed.

　　A great number of stone implements of varied forms and clam shell implements were unearthed in the exploratory excavation of Pojiaohuan site. A small-scaled stone implements making mill was unearthed in the Zuojiang river basin for the first time. The relics unearthed were characteristic of large stone flakes which were quite distinctive in comparison with those from other archaeological sites in the same area and made it a cultural type on its own. The site not only further supplemented the archaeological materials of the neolithic period in the Zuojiang river basin, but also represents a new culture type in the neolithic age in the Zuojiang river basin, which is of great significance.

七、更洒岩洞葬

更洒岩洞葬位于龙州县逐卜乡三
叉村谷更屯东约200米的更洒山上。
2007年3月广西文物保护与考古研究
所会同龙州县博物馆进行实地调查并
对该洞进行了清理，采集到一大批
玉石器、陶器、人牙、人骨残片。玉
石器9件，绝大部分是硅质岩，部分
为玉，计有斧、锛、凿、玦，器形较
小，磨制精致。陶器28件，均为夹细
砂、夹碳陶，不见泥质陶。陶色以灰
黑色、红褐色为主，也有少量灰褐
陶、灰陶。烧制火候普遍较低，器壁
较薄。纹饰绝大多数为细绳纹，仅见
一片为刻划纹。绳纹装饰风格一般为
竖向、斜向，以竖向为主，腹部纹饰
比较规整细密，底部错乱，施纹方法
为竖向、斜向滚压而成。陶器制作方
法均为泥片贴塑，口和领部有轮制痕
迹，绝大多数陶器器内和器表的领部
和肩上部抹有一层细泥浆，有的抹平
且抛光。陶器有圜底器、圈足器，以
圜底器为主，另见有一件平底器。器
形有罐、圈足壶、碗、杯等。圈足壶
和鱼篓形罐比较有特色。墓葬形式与
武鸣先秦岩洞葬相同，陶器部分与大
新歌寿岩、武鸣岜旺岩洞葬的相似，
绝对年代距今3500～3000年。

更洒岩洞葬远景 Distant View of Gengsayan Cave Burial Ground

Ⅶ. Archaeological Site of Gengsayan Cave Burial Ground

The archaeological site of Gengsayan cave burial ground was situated about 200 meters east of Gugeng hamlet of Sancha village of Zhubu township of Longzhou county. In March 2007, Guangxi Institute of Cultural Relics Protection and Archaeology and Longzhou Museum carried out joint field investigation and sorted out the unearthed pieces, including a large number of jade implements, ceramic implements, human teeth as well as human bone bits. Nine jade implements were excavated, most of which were delicately made of silicalite in small forms and in the shapes of axe, adze, chisel and ring. Twenty-eight pieces of ceramic implements were unearthed, which were of coarse ceramics with fine soil and charcoal in grey and brown, but no clay ceramic. The ceramic implements were generally fired in low temperature and of thin texture. The ceramic implements were mostly grey, black and maroon, some of which were gray and brown. Most of the decoration on the implements were thin ropes with only one exception of scratched lines. The rope patterns were mostly vertical and slanting, with the patterns on the side more orderly than those at the bottom. The ceramic implements were all made from clay pieces, with obvious trace of pressing at the mouth and the neck. Some ceramic implements were coated with a layer of fine soil and polished. The ceramic implements were either round at the bottom with vortex or flat at the bottom in the forms of jars, bottles with vortexed bottom, bowls and cups. The ring-leg bottles and the fishbasket-shaped jars were of their own features. The burial remains resembled those excavated in the cave burial ground in Wuming. The ceramic pieces unearthed were similar with those found in Geshouyan mountain in Daxin county and Bawangyan mountain in Wuming county. It was estimated that this site was 3500 to 3000 years ago.

陶器 Ceramic Implement

陶器 Ceramic Implement

陶器 Ceramic Implement

陶器 Ceramic Implement

陶器 Ceramic Implement

陶器 Ceramic Implement

陶器　Ceramic Implement

陶器　Ceramic Implement

陶器　Ceramic Implement

陶器　Ceramic Implement

石器 Stone Implement

石器 Stone Implement

石器 Stone Implement

玉器 Jade Implement

八、庭城遗址

庭城遗址位于广西壮族自治区崇左市龙州县上金乡联江村舍巴屯东北面约500米处，明江、丽江汇流形成的半岛的二级台地上，面积约2600平方米。遗址东南面与上金乡政府隔明江相望，距乡政府约1000米，西北面离舍巴屯台地贝丘遗址约400米，北面与石厂屯隔丽江相望。

遗址略呈椭圆形，四周边缘地势较陡，其西面台地外有一山坡，北面紧临丽江，东、南面一级台地上有一宽阔的平地，明江围绕东、南面平地在三角洲处与丽江交汇，流入左江。平地密密麻麻地种满了甘蔗，从遗址至平地落差为3～5米。该城址地表除村民种植甘蔗外，未遭大的破坏。

庭城遗址远景（东—西）Distant View of the Archaeological Site of Tingcheng(East to West)

庭城遗址全景（南-北）Distant View of the Archaeological Site of Tingcheng(South to North)

Ⅷ. Archaeological Site of Tingcheng

The archaeological site of Tingcheng was located on a second-grade mesa on a peninsular made by Mingjiang river and Lijiang river about 500 meters northeast of Sheba hamlet of Lianjiang village of Shangjin township of Longzhou county in Chongzuo city, covering an area of about 2600 square meters. The site was in the opposite of the seat of local government of Shangjin township on the southeast with a distance of about one kilometer, about 400 meters on the northwest to the shell mould on the mesa in Sheba hamlet, on the opposite of Shichang hamlet on the north.

With an oval shape, the site was surrounded by slope on all sides, with the Lijiang river running on the north, a platform on first-grade mesa on the east and south, the Mingjiang river running around the east and south of the platform and converging with the Lijiang river at the delta. The site was planted with serried sugarcanes, with 3 to 5 meters above the ground. Except for the sugarcane field, the site remained unchanged.

该遗址是在2009年广西第三次全国文物普查左江流域专题调查时被发现的。

为进一步推进花山岩画文化景观申报世界文化遗产工作，2013年和2014年对其各进行了一次试掘，试掘面积约550平方米。发现了三个时期的遗存，包括众多遗迹，大量的建筑材料及少量的石器、陶器、铜器和铁骑等。

The site was discovered in 2009 when the Zuojiang River Basin Research was conducted on the general investigation of the Third National Cutural Relics Census.

As part of the endeavor to promote the application of Zuojiang River Huashan Rock Art Cultural Landscape as World Cultural Heritage, two exploratory excavations were carried out in 2013 and 2014 respectively with an area of about 550 square meters. Relics and remains from three periods were unearthed, including a great amount of architectural waste and some stone implements, ceramic implements, copper implements as well as iron horses.

考古工作者在对庭城遗址进行调查 Trained Personnel Working on the Archaeological Site of Tingcheng

2014年发掘探方分布（局部）Part of the Exploratory Excavation Pits Made in 2014

工作人员在测量 Trained Personnel at Work (gauging)

遗迹清理 Trained Personnel at Work (sorting out the relics)

现场绘图 Trained Personnel at Work (diagraphing)

摄影 Trained Personnel at Work (photographing)

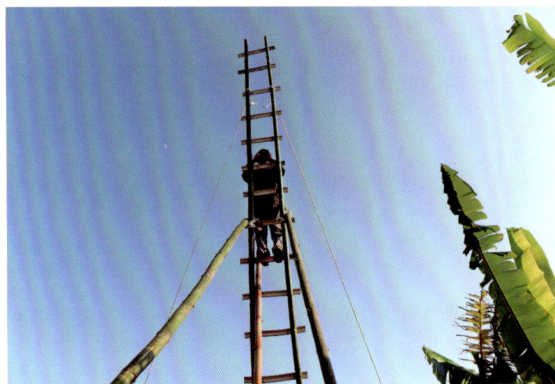

遗迹清理 Trained Personnel at Work (sorting out the relics)

现场观察和清理 Trained Personnel at Work (observing and sorting out relics)

测量 Trained Personnel at Work (gauging)

现场观察和讨论 Trained Personnel at Work (observing and discussing)

TN3E3东壁剖面 The Intersection of the East Side of the Cliff TN3E3

遗址南北区域的地层堆积不完全一致。

2013年发掘北部区域，根据土质、土色及包含物由上而下可统一划分为七层。

The excavated moulds on the north and the south differed.

The north part of the site, which was excavated in 2013, was divided into 7 layers in accordance with the properties, color and contents of the soil.

TG1西壁剖面 The Intersection of the West Side of TG1

2014年发掘的南部区域地层由上而下共分为四层。

The south part of the site, which was excavated in 2014, was divided in four layers.

TS6E1南壁剖面 The Intersection of the South Side of TS6E1

根据地层及出土物判断，该遗址包括三个时期的遗存。

The remains and relics excavated from this site were from three periods in accordance with the condition of the mould and the unearthed contents.

1.第一期遗存

第一期发现少量遗物，可分为陶、石两大类。陶类遗物均为夹砂陶片，夹粗砂，分为红陶、黑陶和灰陶，烧制火候较低，较薄，从残片分析应该为敞口鼓腹的釜罐类器物。石类有磨制石锛、石斧、石网坠、石器半成品、切割痕石块等。

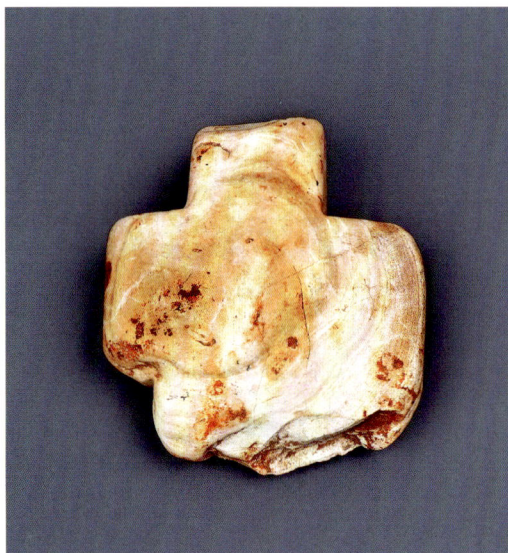

双肩石器 Shoulder-shaped Stone Implement

石璧半成品 A Semi-finished Stone Round Accessory

带切割痕迹的石制品 Stone Implement with Traces of Cutting

石锛毛坯 Rough Cast of Stone Adze

1. Remains from the First Period

A small number of relics were found in the first phase, relics of ceramic and stone implements were found, which were of ceramics and coarse sand and fired in relatively low temperature and in red, black and grey. The broken pieces were thin in texture and part of kettles or jars without lids. Such stone implements as adzes, axes, stone reticulated pendants, semi-finished stone implements and stone chunks with scratched traces were unearthed.

陶片 Ceramic Flakes

陶片 Ceramic Flakes

2.第二期遗存

第二期遗迹包括柱洞、灰坑、散水、弧形带状瓦片分布带、侧插瓦片带等。

2014年发掘区第二期遗迹分布（西南–东北） Overview of the Remains of the Second Period Excavated in 2014 (Southwest to Northeas

2. Remains from the Second Period

Column holes, clay pits, aprolls, tiles in an arc zonal arrangement, erected tiles in zonal arrangement from the second period were found.

柱洞 Column Holes

柱洞底部残留的柱础石 The Base Stones at the Bottom of the Column Holes

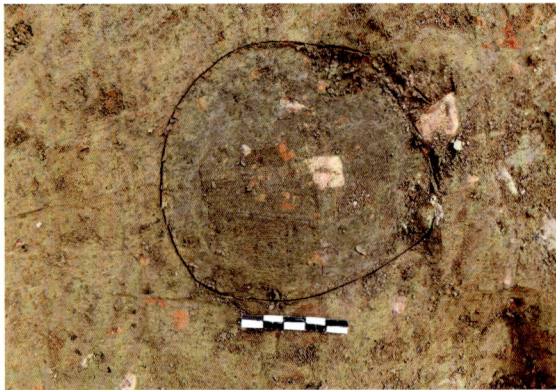

柱洞开口平面 The Opening of the Column Hole

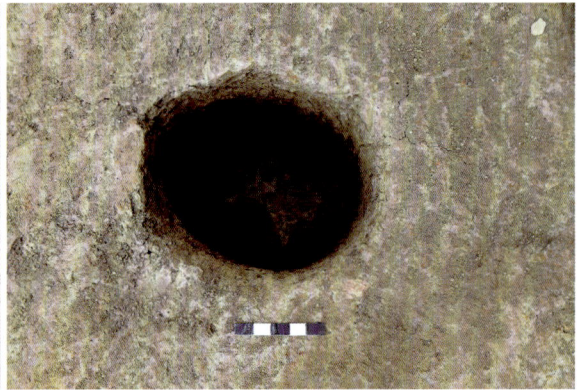

柱洞 Column Hole

灰坑 Clay Pit

灰坑 Clay Pit

灰坑 Clay Pit

灰坑 Clay Pit

散水 Aproll

侧插瓦片带 Erected Tiles in Zonal Arrangement

侧插瓦片带（局部）Part of Erected Tiles in Zonal Arrangement

由东南向西北拍摄

弧形条带状瓦片堆积 Arc Moulds of Tiles in Zonal Arrangement

弧形条带状瓦片堆积(局部) Part of Arc Moulds of Tiles in Zonal Arrangement

第二期遗物主要包括陶、瓷、石、金属制品等。

陶片主要有瓦片、瓦当、网坠、铺首、方格纹戳记陶片、"米"字纹陶片等。

筒瓦 Cylindrical Tile

Excavated relics from the second period mainly included ceramics, porcelains, stone implements, metallic implements, and so on.

Such ceramic implements as tiles, eaves tiles, reticulated pendants, animal head appliques, ceramic pieces with chekered patterns and "米" patterns.

板瓦 Plate Tile

筒瓦 Cylindrical Tile

筒瓦 Cylindrical Tile

板瓦 Plate Tile

带符号筒瓦（内面）The Interior of Cylindrical Tile
with Signals

筒瓦 Cylindrical Tile

瓦当 Eaves Tile

瓦当 Eaves Tile

陶铺首 Ceramic Animal Head Applique

陶片 Ceramic Flake

陶片 Ceramic Flake

陶片 Ceramic Flake

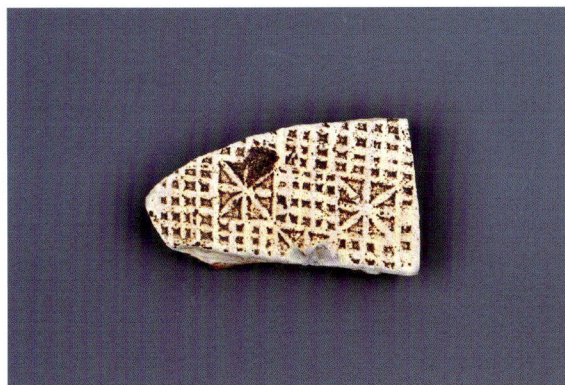

陶片 Ceramic Flake

陶纺轮 Ceramic Weaving Wheel

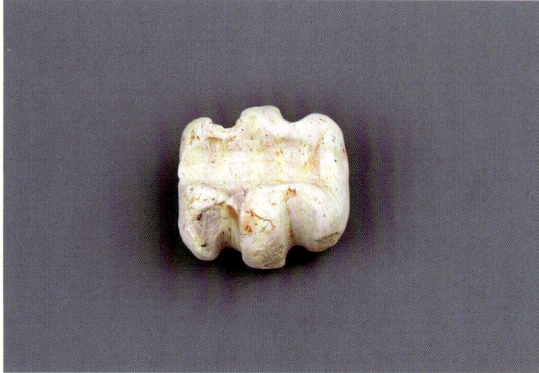

网坠 Reticulated Pendant

陶网坠 Ceramic Reticulated Pendant

陶网坠 Ceramic Reticulated Pendants

铜箭头 Copper Arrow Head

铜箭头 Copper Arrow Heads

铜钺 Copper Tomahawk

第二期石类遗物主要有砺石、砍砸器、石斧、石片、石凿、带切割痕石块等。

Such stone implements as grind stone, choppers, axes, flakes, chisels, chunks with traces of cutting and scratching were unearthed.

砺石 Grind Stone

石凿 Stone Chisel

双肩石器 Shoulder-shaped Stone Implement

3. 第三期遗存

第三期遗迹主要有柱洞、灰坑、沟等。

柱洞 Column Holes

3. Remains from the Third Period

Column Holes, clay pits and trenches from the third period were found.

柱洞 Column Hole

灰坑 Clay Pit

沟和柱洞 Trench and Column Holes

第三期遗物可分为陶、瓷、铁制品等。

板瓦 Plate Tile

筒瓦 Cylindrical Tile

筒瓦 Cylindrical Tile

陶器 Ceramic Implement

陶片 Ceramic Flake

陶片 Ceramic Flake

Ceramics, porcelains, iron implements, and so on, were found in the third period.

陶片 Ceramic Flake

陶片 Ceramic Flake

陶片 Ceramic Flake

陶网坠 Ceramic Reticulated Pendant

陶网坠 Ceramic Reticulated Pendants

铁器 Iron Implement

铁削 Iron Knife

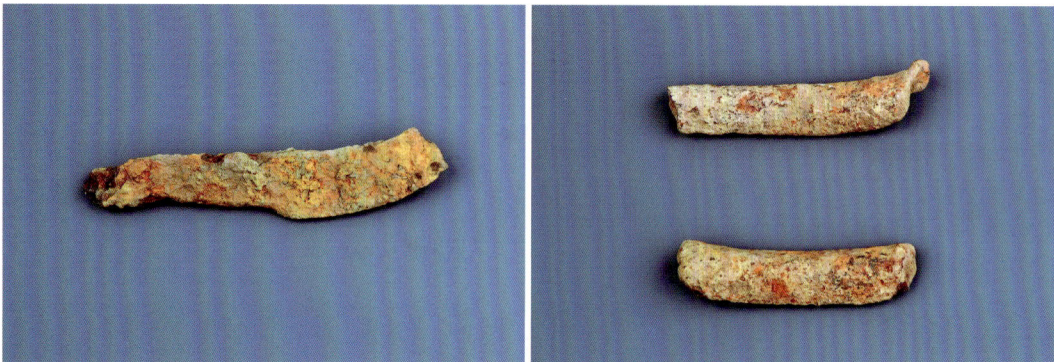

铁器残件 Broken Iron Pieces

第三期遗存包含物中部分器物的时代比较晚，出土的带系器物具有唐宋时代风格，应该为唐宋时期人们生活留下的遗存。第二期遗存包含物具有典型的汉代器物特征，绳纹瓦片与南越国宫署遗址出土的瓦片特征相似，尤其是两地背部的圆形凸点纹特征基本相同。另外，在南越国宫署遗址发现大量云树纹瓦当。陶片中饰"米"字纹、方格纹和"米"字加戳印纹特征具有典型的汉代风格。年代属于西汉时期，距今2000年左右。第一期遗存有石器和夹砂陶片，磨制的双肩石斧制作精美，带切割痕迹的石块质地坚硬，切割痕迹规整。根据地层和遗物综合分析，这一时期遗存应为新石器时代晚期，距今4000～3000年。

庭城遗址堆积的主体是汉代遗存。初步判断，庭城遗址在汉代是一座使用时间较短的带有军事性质的城池。古城池充分利用了三面环水的地理环境，易守难攻。同时，古城池所在位置水路发达，利于信息的传播。古城池规模不大，使用时间不长。

庭城遗址是左江流域首次发现的汉代城址，填补了该地区汉代城址考古的空白，为研究汉代广西西南地区政治、经济、军事、文化等方面的问题提供了宝贵的实物资料。左江流域与花山岩画同时期的古代文化遗址发现不多，这种情况一定程度上限制了岩画的进一步研究。庭城遗址年代清楚，内涵丰富，对于了解岩画产生的历史背景具有重要意义，为花山岩画文化景观申报世界文化遗产申报文本的编制提供了不可或缺的资料。

The unearthed remains from the third period were estimated to descend from the Tang and Song Dynasties, while the unearthed remains from the second period were characteristic of culture of the Han Dynasty, with the tiles decorated with rope patterns, cloud and trees patterns resembling those unearthed from the Nanyue Kingdom Palace which were featured with salient dots arranged in a round manner. Ceramic pieces with 米 patterns, checkered patterns and stamps were discovered which were typical culture of the Western Han Dynasty about 2000 years ago. Stone implements, ceramic pieces with coarse sand, polished shoulder-shaped stone axes and solid stones with cutting traces from the first period were unearthed, which were estimated to descend from the late Neolithic period 4000 to 3000 years ago.

The main part of the Tingcheng site was relics from the Han Dynasty. It was preliminarily estimated that it was built for military purpose at that time. The site was surrounded by water on three sides, which made it a supreme fortress easy to defend but difficult to attack. With convenient canal transportation, information got around readily from the site. However, it was of small scale and served only for a short period.

The archaeological site of Tingcheng was the first city remains descending from the Han Dynasty discovered in Zuojiang river basin, which facilitated the research of Han Dynasty in politics, economics, military affairs and cultural development of the area. Few contemporary culture in Zuojiang river basin developed alongside the Huashan rock paintings, which hindered in-depth research in this regard. With discernible chronological traces and profound cultural significance, the archaeological site of Tingcheng are indispensable resources in compilation of application literature of Huashan rock paintings landscape as world cultural heritage.

广西壮族自治区文化厅领导视察 Officials from Department of Culture of Guangxi Zhuang Autonomous Region Inspecting the Site

龙州县领导视察 Officials of Longzhou County Inspecting the Site

广西壮族自治区文物局领导视察 Officials of Administration of Cultural Heritage of Guangxi Zhuang Autonomous Region Inspecting the Site

专家考察 Experts Inspecting the Site

专家考察 Experts Inspecting the Site

媒体采访 Journalists at Work

媒体采访 Journalists at Work

九、其他零星发现

除了正式考古发掘，龙州还有不少零星发现的器物。从新石器时代到唐宋时期的器物都有，包括石器、陶器、铜器、瓷器等。

Ⅸ. Miscellaneous Findings

Miscellaneous findings including stone implements, ceramic implements, copper implements and porcelains were also unearthed in Longzhou, which could be traced back to the period spanning from neolithic period to the Tang and Song Dynasties.

大石铲（新石器时代）Big Stone Shovel (Neolithic Period)

大石铲（新石器时代）Big Stone Shovel (Neolithic Period)

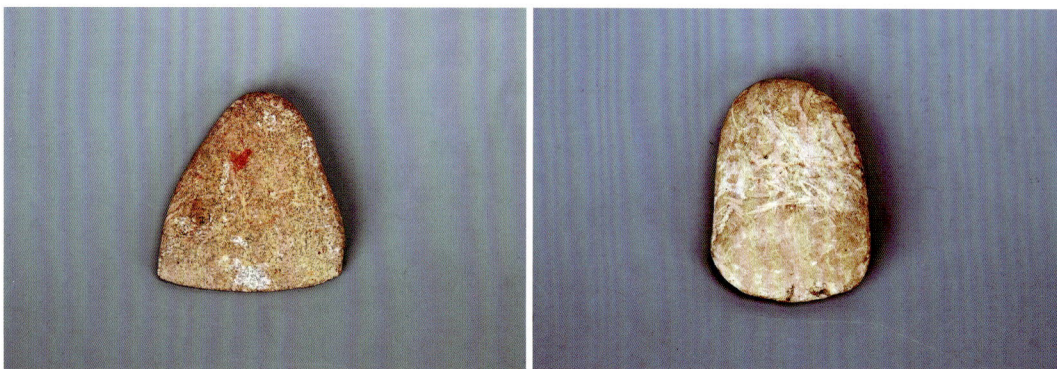

石斧（新石器时代）Stone Axes (Neolithic Period)

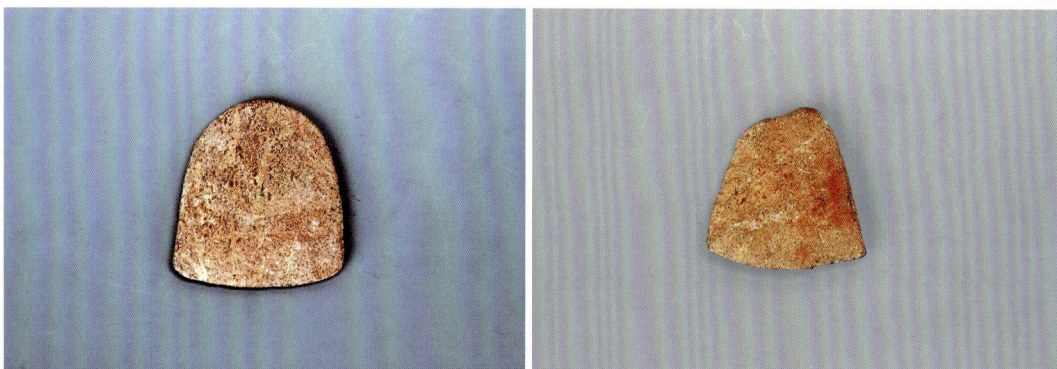

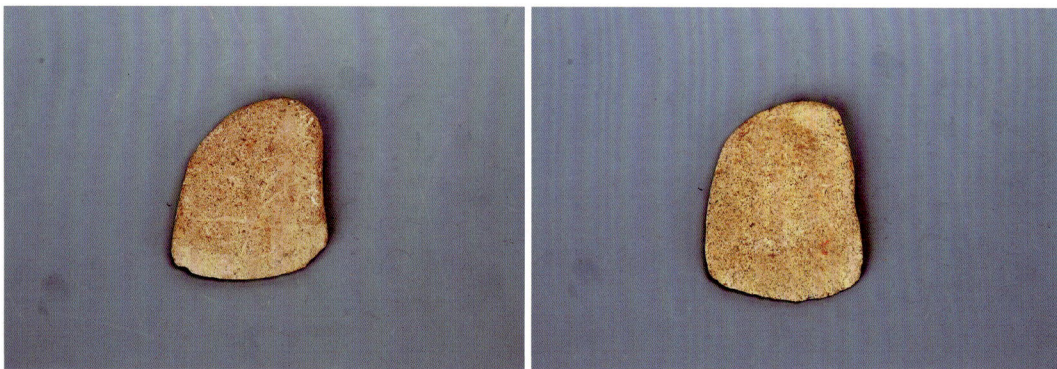

石斧（新石器时代）Stone Axes (Neolithic Period)

石锛（新石器时代）Stone Adzes (Neolithic Period)

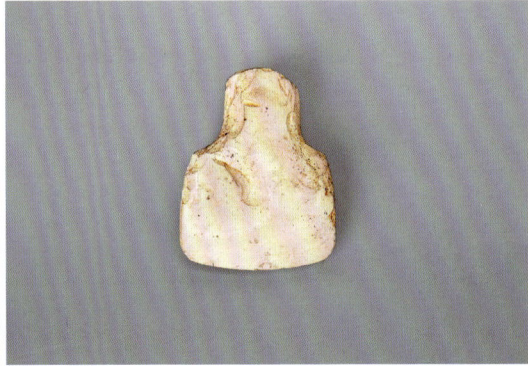

双肩石斧（新石器时代）Shoulder-shaped Axes(Neolithic Period)

双肩石斧（新石器时代）Shoulder-shaped Axes(Neolithic Period)

双肩石斧（新石器时代）Shoulder-shaped Axes(Neolithic Period)

铜剑（战国） Copper Sword (the Warring States Period)

铜鼓（汉代） Bronze Drum (the Han Dynasty)

瓷瓶（宋代） Porcelain Bottle (the Song Dynasty)

四系罐（宋代） Four-ear Jar (the Song Dynasty)

考古学视野下的古代龙州

Part Three   Ancient Longzhou in the Archaeological Perspective

龙州的考古工作起步不算太晚，但发展一直比较缓慢。长期以来，我们对龙州历史的认识多停留在近现代革命史上，对古代龙州认识很少。近年来通过考古调查与发掘，我们对龙州的历史有了近现代革命史上，对古代龙全新的认识。通过考古学家的研究和解读，那一个个遗址、一件件标本，为我们勾勒了一幅幅古代龙州的历史画卷。

1. 龙州历史悠久，古代文化发达

虽然目前在龙州还没有发现旧石器时代遗址，但是考古学者们在县城附近的地层剖面中发现了很多玻璃陨石，这为我们寻找旧石器遗址提供了重要线索。

目前的发现表明，至少在距今7000年，龙州就有了较大规模的人类活动。考古工作者在龙州大地上发现了大量新石器时代遗址。新石器时代遗址以贝丘遗址为主，包含的遗物很丰富。从发掘的材料来看，龙州贝丘遗址区域特征明显：地层中含有大量螺壳及水、陆生动物遗骸，生产工具以打制石器、磨制石器共存为主，部分遗址出土的琢边石器特色鲜明。蚌器数量较多，有的遗址双肩蚌铲精美，锯齿刃蚌器很有特色。发现少量骨器，陶器使用很少，有的遗址甚至不见陶片。由此可以判断，当时龙州气候温暖湿润，野生动植物资源丰富，人们已经学会了制作各种石器、蚌器和骨器，会上山打猎、羡渊而渔，过着平等的原始生活，死后按照本地的风俗进行安葬。他们用勤劳的双手创造出有别于其他地区的文化。

新石器时代晚期，龙州开始出现岩洞葬；先秦时期，岩洞葬盛行。岩洞葬埋葬形式独特，出土的器物特征鲜明，反映了某些特殊人群的精神世界，是某种独特的文化现象，标志着当时社会分化开始加剧。

龙州发现的无名山遗址二期和庭城遗址等是汉代的文化遗存。庭城遗址是左江流域发现的唯一的汉代城址，两次试掘出土了大量的建筑构件和建筑遗迹，是一座具有军事性质的城池，其重要性不言而喻。庭城遗址的发现，表明当时龙州已经处于中央的管辖范围之内，汉文化已经深入到了这里，但大部分村落应该仍然保留着自己的传统文化。

后期历代遗存的发现，表明龙州经济社会得到了很大的发展，同时也表明龙州大部分时间处于政府的管理之中，但这种管理多数是通过当地的酋长或者土官来完成，整个社会维持着相当程度的自治。

总的来说，从石器时代开始一直到明清时期，龙州地区文化的发展延绵不断，不仅遗址数量多、类型多样，而且出土的遗物也很丰富。这些都说明龙州地区历史悠久，古代文化灿烂。

Archaeology in Longzhou county was initiated at an early age, however it has been underdeveloped. Knowledge about the county has been limited to the modern revolutionary history. Archaeological investigation and excavation in recent years have broadened our horizon on the knowledge of the county in ancient times. We get a glimpse of the cornucopia of the little town through every single site and unearthed piece which were interpreted by experts.

1. Longzhou Enjoys A Long History with Glamorous Culture

Though no sites from the Paleolithic period has been discovered in Longzhou by far, the large amount of tektites discovered in the stratigraphic section around the town made significant clue for the existence of remains from that period.

The unearthed relics demonstrate that Longzhou had a larger scale of human activities at least 7000 years ago. A great amount of sites from the Neolithic period were excavated in this area, most of which were shell moulds with varied relics. The excavated relics are of characteristic of this region, with a large number of aquatic and terrestrial snails and animal remains, forged and polished stone implements and some stone implements with delicately chiseled edge contained in the mould. The unearthed clam shell implements were abound in number, with delicately made shoulder-shaped clam shell shovels and serried-edged clam shell knives. A few bone implements were found, and few, or none ceramic implements were discovered in some sites. The climate at that time was mild and moisture with abundant animals and plantation. People inhabiting in this area at that time had learned to make various kinds of stone implements, clam shell implements and bone implements. They led a primitive human life on hunting and fishing. Burial rituals were performed in accordance with local customs at that time. Hard-working people in this area created distinctive culture.

Cave burial appeared in the late Neolithic period, which became popular in the pre-Qin period. As a special burial format, cave burial mirrored the mental state of certain class, with characteristic unearthed relics shedding light on the rapid stratification of social classes at that time.

The archaeological sites of Wuming Mountain and Tingcheng descended from the Han Dynasty, the latter of which was the only of its kind in Zuojiang river basin and used to be a military fortress. The existence of the archaeological site of Tingcheng lent testimony to the overall governance of the central government at that time, with culture of Han nationality was popular in the area and coexisting with local culture.

Unearthed relics from different periods show that Longzhou enjoyed certain autonomy and developed in a orderly manner for most of the time under the leadership of local governors.

Cultural line in Longzhou was continuous from the Stone Age to the Ming and Qing Dynasties, which finds testimony in the various excavated sites and relics.

2. 古代龙州考古学文化地域特征鲜明，为本地族群所创造

龙州地区新石器时代中期的贝丘遗址众多，尽管文化面貌与周边其他文化有一定的联系，但地域特征明显。如极少发现陶器，流行双肩蚌铲，使用锯齿刃蚌器。在石器方面，打制石器与磨制石器并存，打制石器占多数，磨制石器制作时流行利用扁平砾石为原料先对四周进行加工然后再进行磨制的传统。可以确定，龙州地区的贝丘遗址大部分具有本地特色。我们可以把以宝剑山A洞遗址第一期遗存为代表的考古学文化称为"宝剑山文化"。

从新石器时代晚期开始至先秦时期，龙州地区的地域特点更加明显，其大体特征是：石器主要为磨制的有肩石器，磨制精美，用料考究；陶器是以夹细砂的灰褐或红褐色陶为主，器表装饰细绳纹、绳纹和刻划水波组合纹、刻划曲线，陶器烧制的火候较高，薄胎，为手工制作，绳纹多为滚压的交错细绳纹，相当一部分在绳纹上再施"S"形多线刻划纹，流行圜底器和圈足器，器形以高领、圜底的釜、罐为主。流行岩洞葬。

如果我们要寻找骆越文化的踪迹，那么龙州地区发现的这些很有特色的遗存将是绝对不可忽视的材料。

2. In the Archaeological Perspective, Culture in Ancient Longzhou Was Distinct and Developed by Local People at that Time

Shell moulds from the mid Neolithic period were of characteristic of Longzhou area, which were distinctive with shoulder-shaped shovels, serried-edged clam shell implements, forged and polished stone implements. Polished stone implements at that time were made of flat gravel in a traditional way that the edge was first processed and then polished. The remains of Baojian Mountain (First Period) were recognized as Baojian Mountain Culture in archaeological terms.

Features of this area from the late Neolithic period to the pre-Qin period were more obvious. Stone implements in this area were mostly delicately polished shoulder-shaped implements. The unearthed ceramic implements, hand-made and grilled at fairly high temperature, were mostly grey and brown with fine sand, decorated with fine rope patterns which were mostly rolling interlaced ones and on some of which were scratched with "S" shaped patterns, scratched wave patterns, scratched curves on the surface and in the forms of utensils with round flat bottoms and wund legs. Cave burials were popular in the area during the above-mentioned period.

The excavated relics and remains of Longzhou were indispensible clue to Luoyue culture, which we are endeavoring to probe into.

3.古代龙州考古学文化是一种开放的文化，在自身发展的过程中，不断与周边文化进行交流。龙州考古学文化与邕江流域、右江流域等在文化面貌上具有很多相似的地方

3. Longzhou Culture in the Archaeological Perspective,

which Resembled Those in Yongjiang River Basin and Youjiang River Basin and So On, was Open and Dynamic and Mixing with Its Counterparts in Surrounding Areas.

4. 古代龙州地区从新石器时代晚期（即距今5000～4000年）开始了社会复杂化进程，社会从简单迈向复杂

龙州地区到了新石器时代晚期，开始出现社会复杂化趋势，出现了以大石铲为代表的高度发达的文化。大石铲器物形体硕大，器身扁薄，棱角分明，制作规整，许多器物无使用痕迹，特征极为明显。学者们普遍认为，大石铲是一种祭祀遗存。大石铲的存在显示当时已经出现了礼制和明显的社会分化，出现了比较严密的社会组织结构。先秦时期岩洞葬被认为是高等级人群的特殊墓葬，随葬的精美磨制双肩石器无使用痕迹，显示了墓主身份的高贵，表明当时社会开始出现了贫富分化现象。

4. Ever since the Late Neolithic Age about 5000 to 4000 Years Ago, Social Development in the Area of Longzhou Became Complicated.

Social complication symbolized by big stone shovels appeared in the late Neolithic period. Big stone shovels were delicately made, thin and angular, most of which remained unused. It is universally recognized by experts that the big stone shovels served sacrificial and ritual purposes. The existence of big stone shovels lends testimony to the speculation that rituals and social strata came into being at that time. Cave burials from the pre-Qin period were considered to be resting places of the noble with delicately made shoulder-shaped stone implements without traces of use, which shed some light on the polarization of the rich and the poor.

后记

　　龙州，风景优美，人杰地灵。这里不仅在近现代孕育了光辉灿烂的红色文化和商业文化，而且在远古时期就创造了璀璨的古代文明。

　　经过考古工作者的不懈努力，龙州悠久的历史和发达的古代文化正逐步清晰地展现在我们的面前。考古工作的开展，离不开各级部门和领导的支持。国家文物局、广西壮族自治区文化厅、广西壮族自治区文物局、中共龙州县委员会、龙州县人民政府以及相关乡镇机关单位都对龙州考古提供了有力的支持和帮助。对于近年来一直在龙州从事考古工作的我们来说，这是十分欣慰的事情。在这里，我们对各级领导的关心和支持表示感谢。同时，还要感谢广西文物保护与考古研究所、崇左壮族博物馆、梧州博物馆、广西师范大学、南宁博物馆、龙州纪念馆等业务单位的领导和同事，他们为龙州的考古工作提供了不遗余力的帮助。

　　本书在编写过程中还得到了黄伟、麻超君、李秋健、李珍、谢广维、黄鑫、黄强、蒲晓东、刘芸、李光亮、潘俊杰、张玉艳、陈紫茹等同志的支持，在此一并表示感谢。尤其要感谢的是，李珍和谢广维分别提供了更洒岩洞葬和舍巴遗址的材料。

　　由于是初步整理且水平有限，本书错误在所难免，望各位批评指正。

编者

2017年10月13日

Postscript

With picturesque scenery that nurtures generation after generation of talents, Longzhou boasts glamorous ancient culture as well as revolutionary and commercial culture.

A panoramic view of the ancient culture of Longzhou was unrolled owing to unremitting efforts of trained personnel in archaeological field. The archaeological research would not have yielded such fruitful results without support from such departments as State Administration of Cultural Heritage, Department of Culture of Guangxi Zhuang Autonomous Region, Administration of Cultural Heritage of Guangxi, CPC Longzhou Committee, Municipal Government of Longzhou as well as relevant departments on township levels. We are grateful to all the support that had come in various ways. Gratitude also goes to Guangxi Institute of Cultural Relics Protection and Archaeology, Chongzuo Museum of Zhuang Nationality, Wuzhou Museum, Guangxi Normal University, Nanning Museum, and Longzhou Memorial Museum.

We would like to extend heartfelt thanks to Huang Wei, Ma Chaojun, Li Qiujian, Li Zhen, Xie Guangwei, Huang Xin, Huang Qiang, Pu Xiaodong, Liu Yun, Li Guangliang, Pan Junjie, Zhang Yuyan, Chen Ziru. Especially thanks go to Li Zhen and Xie Guangwei for their contribution of literature on Gengsayan cave burial ground and Sheba site.

The present literature is the preliminary research in this regard and subject to rectification.

Authors
Oct 13, 2017